BLAKES

BLAKES

PHOTOGRAPHY BY SIMON GRIFFIT

ANDREW BLAKE

HAMLYN

First published 1996 by William Heinemann Australia

Reprinted 1997 by Hamlyn Australia
a part of Reed Books Australia
35 Cotham Road, Kew, Victoria 3101
a division of Reed International Books Australia Pty Ltd

Copyright text © Andrew Blake, 1996
Copyright photographs © Simon Griffiths, 1996

All rights reserved. Without limiting the rights under copyright above, no part of this publication may be reproduced, stored in or introduced into a retrieval system, or transmitted in any form or by any means (electronic, mechanical, photocopying, recording or otherwise), without prior written permission of both the copyright owner and the publisher.

National Library of Australia
  Cataloguing-in-Publication data:

Blake, Andrew, 1959- .
    Blakes

    Includes index.
    ISBN 0 947334 74 2
    1. Cookery. 2. Restaurants - Victoria - Melbourne.
    I. Title.

641.509

Designed by Grant Slaney, The Modern Art Production Group
Produced in China by Mandarin Offset

CONTENTS

LIST OF RECIPES VII INTRODUCTION 1
WINE AND FOOD MATCHING 3
THE RECIPES 5 BLAKES BASICS 158
ACKNOWLEDGEMENTS 168 INDEX 169

LIST OF RECIPES

1. Tuna carpaccio on shaved fennel with preserved lemon & sevruga caviar — 6
2. Crisped Sydney rock oysters with chilli pickled lettuce & ginger sauce — 7
3. Wood-fire roasted Pacific oysters with wasabi butter & brioche crumbs — 8
4. Steamed pink-eye chat potatoes with caviars & an oyster shooter — 9
5. Roast Spring Bay scallops with tomato & cucumber salsa — 14
6. Caesar salad — 15
7. Chilled roasted tomato soup with yabbies & avocado — 16
8. Chilled cauliflower soup with curry cream & shucked oysters — 18
9. King crab & bbq pork ricepaper rolls with tamarind sauce — 19
10. Tuna tartare with eggplant crisps & coriander oil — 20
11. Char-grilled asparagus with chopped egg & parmesan oil — 21
12. Lobster salad with broad beans, smoked tomatoes & beet dressing — 26
13. Goat's cheese, fennel & olive tart with red pepper sauce — 27
14. Red pepper terrine with a mussel & watercress salad — 28
15. Roast veal with tuna mayo & stewed peppers — 29
16. Smoked salmon stack with pickled cucumber, horseradish & lattice chips — 34
17. Ocean trout gravlax with grilled corncakes & snowpea foliage — 35
18. BBQ king prawns with eggplant–haloumi fritters, tabouleh & turmeric oil — 36
19. Yabbie salad with gazpacho sauce & galette potato — 38
20. Twice-baked roast garlic soufflé with parsley sauce & sautéd snails — 39
21. BBQ salmon nicoise salad — 40
22. Marinated young leeks with crab remoulade — 41
23. Gratinee of young artichokes with mud crab & tomato salsa — 46
24. Seared sardine fillets with a tomato–fennel stew & green olive tapenade — 47
25. Pumpkin tortellini with mustard fruits & citrus butter — 48
26. Asparagus & fontina tortelli with vegetable essence & truffle oil — 49
27. Prawn & basil ravioli with a smoked tomato sauce — 54
28. Vegetable fritto misto with tapenade, aioli & hummus — 55
29. Crisped zucchini flowers stuffed with goat's cheese ricotta on ratatouille — 56
30. Chilli corn soup with steamed clams — 58
31. Jerusalem artichoke soup with yabbies & sautéd apple — 59
32. Squab minestrone with gruyère toasts — 60
33. Curried dhal soup with seared scallops & coriander yoghurt — 61
34. Char-grilled baby octopus on char-grilled vegetables with a balsamic drizzle — 66
35. Coulibiac of Atlantic salmon with chive beurre blanc & salmon roe — 67
36. Potato, artichoke & mascarpone pie — 68
37. Saffron potato gnocchi with clams & asparagus — 69
38. Grilled duck cakes with a chilli–mango salsa — 74
39. Sage pappardelle with duck ragout & olives — 75
40. Beetroot risotto with kangaroo prosciutto — 76
41. Roast quail & spring pea risotto — 77
42. Blackened quail with a green pawpaw salad — 82
43. BBQ quail with zucchini fritters & thyme hollandaise — 83
44. Potato pancakes with sweetbreads & morels — 84
45. Duck & wild mushroom pastie with white bean mash — 86
46. Roast duck breast on turnip purée with spiced pear — 87

47.	Seared salt-cured salmon on potatoes mashed with truffle oil	88
48.	Sardine pizza with grilled eggplant & tapenade	89
49.	Moreton Bay bug pizza with coriander pesto	94
50.	Grilled calf's liver on pommes sarladaise with smoky baba ghannouj	95
51.	Quail sausage roll with verjus sauce	96
52.	Wild mushroom fricassée with smoked hare & polenta	102
53.	Parmesan-crumbed calf's liver with gorgonzola & silverbeet	103
54.	BBQ tuna steak with a warm potato salad & salsa verde	104
55.	Whole deep-fried baby snapper with three-flavoured sauce & root crisps	105
56.	Steamed wild barramundi on a basil risotto with red pepper essence	110
57.	Pistachio crusted blue-eye cod with saffron mashed potatoes & masala sauce	111
58.	Paillard of chicken breast with preserved lemon couscous & pistachio butter	112
59.	'Baked in a bag' chicken breast with prosciutto & braised witlof	113
60.	Hazelnut-crumbed veal cutlets with eggplant relish	118
61.	Roast lamb loin with white beans & mint pesto	119
62.	Peppered ox fillet with horseradish mashed potatoes	120
63.	BBQ fillet of beef with gorgonzola polenta & red onion jam	122
64.	Paillard of kangaroo with sweet potato mash & red pepper chutney	123
65.	Venison burger with grilled pineapple & chilli mayo	124
66.	Red Thai peanut kangaroo curry with coconut rice	125
67.	Sage-roasted chicken breast with goat's cheese gnocchi	130
68.	Roast duck with sweet potato mash, bok choy & bittersweet orange sauce	131
69.	Baked ham hock with spicy baked beans & pickled okra	132
70.	Little pavs with clotted cream, wild strawberries & rose syrup	133
71.	Gratinee of berries with a sabayon	136
72.	Banana & frangipane cream pizza with honey ice-cream	137
73.	Fig & raspberry tart with toasted almond ice-cream	138
74.	Blackberry shortcake with lemon cream	139
75.	Hot blood plum soufflé with blood plum ice-cream	144
76.	Mandarin & cardamom brûlée	145
77.	Caramelised pear pizza with mascarpone	146
78.	Profiteroles with pistachio ice-cream & hot mocha sauce	147
79.	White chocolate & dried blueberry ice-cream 'kreem between'	152
80.	Hot butter waffles with grilled peaches, vanilla bean ice-cream & raspberry sauce	153
81.	Bread & butter pudding	154
82.	Poonie's icky sticky date & chocolate pudding with butterscotch sauce	155

INTRODUCTION

Nearly twenty years ago, an uncle asked if I was interested in starting an apprenticeship in cooking. Although I had dabbled in cooking in my early teens, to the extent of baking pavlovas and cheesecakes for friends of my mother, I had never considered it as a possible career. But I grew into an adolescent with a voracious appetite, and an understanding that my mother was not a good cook, and decisions became a whole lot easier.

Most cooks wax lyrical of early memories, watching their mothers and grandmothers in quiet awe, as they lovingly prepared homely food for the family table. My early memories are of the sound of carbon being scraped off burnt toast, or chewing endlessly on a roast topside cooked in a Sunbeam electric frypan for hours. I thank my mother for a bizarre form of encouragement to pursue a career in food.

Following an apprenticeship – which taught me very little about real food – I applied for a cook's position at Fanny's, which was a leading Melbourne restaurant at that time, and had been for some twenty years. I feel as though this was my true apprenticeship as Fanny's was where I really learnt about cooking and food style. For this I am eternally grateful to Gloria Staley. The Staley family, who owned Fanny's, pulled together a remarkable group of cooks at that time. Today, fifteen years on, we still get together occasionally, have a drink and look back at the camaraderie that was Fanny's kitchen.

In 1985, I was given the opportunity to start the kitchen at the Staleys' new restaurant in Sydney, Chez Oz. This is where things started to get serious for me. In the mid 80s, the Sydney press treated chefs very differently from their Melbourne counterparts. Sydney food critics, Leo Schofield in particular, promoted chefs rather than the restaurateurs. As much as it was great to be recognised and praised, I believe things went a little too far. Some chefs started to take themselves too seriously. After all, we are just tradesmen who enjoy what we do.

In 1988, I left Chez Oz for Arthur's. For the first time in my cooking life, I had complete autonomy over the food I cooked. What I tried to do at Arthur's, in conjunction with my good friend Glenn Davies, was to break down customers' normal dining habits. We created a menu where dishes ran from light through to heavy and tried to take away the 'entree, main, one potato, three veg.' way of thinking. People started to share dishes, so that they enjoyed more flavour sensations. It was also an unpretentious way of eating; something more akin to eating at home. Breaking the bread and all that kind of thing.

I discovered over this first year of 'freedom' that I was getting further and further away from my cooking 'roots'. Having the respect and support of your peers means more to a cook than the best critique. We were doing interesting things with produce that was drastically improving. Everything became very exciting. Whilst in this developmental stage, not every dish was a winner, but the most important thing was the development.

There was one very important aspect to the change in my cooking direction. In my training, and by this I include Fanny's, everything we cooked was very labour-intensive and supposed to be produced by a kitchen that had a large staff. But only five-star hotels and premium restaurants – where 12–15 kitchen staff cook for 60 people – can afford such brigades. Why were we trying to reproduce this kind of food with four or five people in the kitchen?

My food became a lot less handled and lot more pure in nature. Five years before, I would have taken some asparagus, cooked it, puréed it, added cream and gelatine to it, and then set it in a mould. Now I would steam it, grill it or fry it and do a bit of simple but effective value-adding to it – as long as it subtly enhanced the original glory of the asparagus.

After Arthur's, I returned to Melbourne and worked for the Kanis cousins at Cafe Kanis. We three then created Kanis, Blake and Kanis, in an attempt to sell restaurant-style food to the eat-at-home market. It was a lot of hard work for very little return, but I still enjoyed the product and the challenge.

Then, in 1991, I was approached by the powers-that-be of the soon-to-be-completed Southgate complex on the Yarra River. I had no money, but I had an idea. Management liked it and somehow I got Blakes started. At last, my very own restaurant!

I still remember signing cheques on our first day; cheques to the value of $9,000 more than I had in the bank. That was on a Friday, and on the Monday morning, I banked $12,000. The rest is history.

Part of my idea for Blakes was to get right back to basics. In the kitchen we had a wood-burning oven, a wood-burning char-grill, and a wood-burning fireplace for a rotisserie. Using these, along with other more conventional cooking equipment, I felt as though we could cook the kind of food that people would love. The architect, Peter Maddison, had created a space that enhanced my food, and today, four years later, I still love my restaurant.

Blakes wine list and suggested wine/food matchings, including those in this book, come from champion sommelier Grant Van Every. I've known Grant since my Sydney days and he taught me about the matching of food and wine, and how one can open up and complement the other. It was a real coup for the restaurant that Grant accepted my invitation to move to Melbourne to run the wine side of the business. He has an amazing palate, and a desire to share it with anyone willing to take the time to listen to his amazingly boring story of his one and only hole-in-one!

This book is a collection of the most popular dishes of mine; some created years prior to Blakes being. For the most part, they are deceptively easy for home cooks to reproduce. You will not be bamboozled by technique. Basic kitchen skills and basic kitchen equipment are all that is required. Although the names of the recipes sometimes reflect the produce I use in my kitchen – Coffin Bay scallops or king crab, for instance – don't be put off trying them if you can't buy exactly the same ingredient. Just substitute the best and freshest produce available to you.

To use this book, just imagine it is one of my menus, starting at the lightest dish and ending at the heaviest. The recipes are all intended to feed four people. Please enjoy.

P.S. My mother is now a very good cook.

WINE AND FOOD MATCHING

Wine has been made for thousands of years. We know that since Roman times winemakers have realised the varying qualities of different varieties, vineyards and vintages. The development of cuisine – as opposed to the cooking of food for sustenance – has an equally long history. In Europe traditionally the great food regions have also been the great wine-producing regions. The very heart of gastronomy is a plate of sublime food perfectly complemented by a glass of wine. I know when I taste such a match, but due to the complex nature of the process when the wine and food combine it is very difficult to translate this affinity into words.

A feature of the Blakes' menus has been that with each dish a wine has been suggested. The decisions initially were arrived at through trial and error, in many cases I relied on my 'gut instinct'. I have had some spectacular failures, but by and large the combinations work. The general feedback has been that customers have been encouraged to try the combinations and taste wines for the first time, so discovering new wineries and varieties.

The process I use to match the food and wine has become more methodical and reliable over years of experience. In time I hope that some of the combinations will become classic – as indeed so will many of the dishes, no doubt.

Appreciating wine is subjective and very individual. I will not attempt to tell you how to evaluate wine; after all, this is a cookbook and there are many excellent books and courses that are devoted to the subject. I do have one piece of advice, though. When you select a wine to match food you must try to avoid the preferences and habits you have developed.

How do you select the right wine for a particular dish? Break down the components of the wine in the following manner and you will find it easier to find the perfect (or as close to perfect as possible) match. This is how I generally go about the selection process.

Assessing the wine
First, taste the wine and assess it for three qualities: flavour, texture and finish.

Flavour
You will find that most wine tastes of fruit. Look for the primary fruit characters. There are a range of flavours: riesling is like citrus fruit, sauvignon blanc like passionfruit with a herbal grassy overlay, chardonnay like stonefruit and melon. Red wines have similarly distinctive fruit characters: pinot noir like strawberries and plums, shiraz like raspberries and cabernet sauvignon is like black currants. Of course, this is an oversimplification and every wine will have a different balance of fruit characters.

The next thing to do is to assess the secondary flavours. These are usually the result of winemaking procedures. The wine may have a new oak flavour or a nutty and caramel character from the barrel and malolactic fermentation. In well-made, balanced wine these characters support but do not dominate the fruit of the wine. They are, however, important in selecting the wine to match food.

Texture
This is a factor often overlooked in assessing wines, but it is critical when matching with food. The weight of a wine in the mouth and its texture varies with the grape variety, winemaking technique and the level of alcohol. Some varieties, such as sauvignon blanc, always seem light and fresh in the mouth, whilst chardonnay is far richer and more viscous. Some wines may feel creamy and buttery, whilst certain reds develop a fleshy or meaty texture in the mouth.

Finish
The finish of a wine is a balance of three components: acid, sugar and tannin. Tannin, which results from the juice being allowed to macerate with grape

skins and stalks, is basically only a factor in red wine (although some barrel-aged whites display wood tannin). The sugar is a combination of the ripe fruit character and residual sugar (unfermented sugar). The acid occurs naturally in the fruit, and is predominantly tartaric acid; white wines can have a higher proportion than reds of the crisp and harder malic acid, or the soft and creamy lactic acid if malolactic fermentation has occurred.

Assessing the food
To match the food to the wine you must assess it in the same manner that you analyse the wine. Chefs have a little more freedom than winemakers, there is virtually no limit to what they can add to a dish or how they may prepare it. This makes for exciting and innovative combinations of ingredients but can result in tastes that are difficult to describe.

Flavour
The taste of each meat and fish varies and this will require consideration when finding the appropriate wine match. Assess the aroma, particularly the herbs and spices that have been used, and the effects of the cooking procedures.

Texture
Decide if there are components in the dish that will make it grainy or starchy. Also decide on how much sauce, or jus, is incorporated into the dish.

Finish
In most dishes the finish will be similar to wine in that it will generally be dominated by acid or sweetness (we would have to blame the chef if the finish was bitter). Some foods that have a high fat or oil content will mask these acid or sweet characters at the finish. It is paramount in these situations to find a wine that can balance the finish.

Matching food and wine
Now the matching process takes place.

Flavour
Look for flavours that match or are complementary. Aromatic whites, such as riesling and sauvignon blanc, are best suited to highly spiced foods, whilst the subtle character of chardonnay is better suited to more delicately flavoured food.

It is also important to try and match the intensity of flavour. Big, intensely flavoured food simply swamps meek, delicate wines and vice versa.

Texture
With texture try to find contrasts. Butter-based sauces or oily dressings are best matched with crisp, fresh wines that cut through the richness. An exception – and there are always exceptions – is game or strongly flavoured red meats. Here it is advisable to find a wine that is powerful and has a meaty or fleshy texture itself.

Finish
The overriding consideration here is balance. Food that is acidic should be balanced with wine that is slightly sweet. Oily or fatty food should be matched with wine that is either crisp with acid (whites) or firm with tannin (reds). The finish of the wine will bring the whole combination into balance.

Each recipe in this book has a recommended style of wine. But not for a moment do I suggest that this is the only one you should consider. In fact I urge you to try different wines with a dish so you can find the perfect match for your palate. I have not specified particular labels, vintages or regions. This would be too narrow in its scope and far too easy for you. Seek expert advice on wine if you are not sure what particular wines taste like. Specialist fine wine stores all are staffed by experienced, knowledgeable wine lovers. If you are in a restaurant ask for the assistance of the sommelier, who not only knows the wine on the list but has a deep understanding of the restaurant's food.

Grant Van Every

THE RECIPES

1. TUNA CARPACCIO ON SHAVED FENNEL WITH PRESERVED LEMON & SEVRUGA CAVIAR

ingredients

1 medium fennel bulb
2 teaspoons finely diced preserved lemon (p.162)
50 ml (1½ fl oz) extra-virgin olive oil
juice of 1 lime
freshly ground black pepper
200 g (6½ oz) sashimi-quality tuna
30 g (1 oz) sevruga caviar
2 teaspoons chopped chives
40 ml (1¼ fl oz) white truffle oil

method

Cut the fennel bulb in half and remove the core. Shave the fennel very finely and blanch in boiling water for 20 seconds. Refresh under running cold water, drain and pat dry. Put in a bowl and add preserved lemon, oil and lime juice. Let sit for 10 minutes and season with pepper.

Cut tuna into 4 even pieces. Flatten each piece between 2 sheets of lightly oiled plastic wrap using the side of a meat cleaver – this must be done very carefully so as not to tear or damage the flesh. The tuna should be reddish and paper-thin to qualify for its 'carpaccio' tag.

Spread the dressed fennel evenly over 4 serving plates. Place tuna carefully over the fennel. Smatter with caviar and chives.

Drizzle over the white truffle oil. To add a bit of theatre, do this with an eye-dropper at the table. The oil is so pungent, this tiny amount is all that is necessary.

MATURE SPARKLING WINE WITH EXTENDED LEES CONTACT. THE YEASTY CHARACTER WILL MATCH PERFECTLY WITH THE CAVIAR AND TRUFFLE OIL, WHILST THE DELICATE NATURE OF THE FRUIT WILL NOT OVERPOWER THE SUBTLE FLAVOUR OF THE FISH. THE TINGLE FROM THE EFFERVESCENCE WILL PROVIDE TEXTURAL CONTRAST.

2. CRISPED SYDNEY ROCK OYSTERS WITH CHILLI PICKLED LETTUCE & GINGER SAUCE

ingredients

32 oysters - removed from shell and shell reserved
1 cos lettuce
500 g (1 lb) rocksalt
plain flour
1 quantity beer batter (p.163)

pickling liquid
250 ml (8 fl oz) white wine vinegar
100 g (3½ oz) sugar
2 shallots
3 bird's-eye chillies
2 cloves garlic
3 bay leaves

ginger sauce
100 g sugar
30 ml (1 fl oz) white wine vinegar
150 ml (5 fl oz) white wine
150 ml (5 fl oz) water
1 x 2.5 cm (1 in) knob ginger
1 tablespoon soy sauce
1 tablespoon cornflour

method

Combine all pickling liquid ingredients in a non-corrosive saucepan and simmer for 10 minutes. Strain and pour over cos lettuce that has been washed, dried and shredded. Store in a glass jar for at least two days before using.

To make the ginger sauce, combine the sugar and vinegar in a small heavy saucepan, allow sugar to dissolve, then caramelise over high heat (the syrup should start turning a caramel brown). On reaching the caramel stage, add the white wine and water and reduce heat to a gentle simmer. Finely slice the knob of ginger and add to saucepan along with the soy. Leave saucepan on the lowest temperature possible for about 30 minutes. Wet the cornflour with a little cold water to form a smooth liquid, add a little of this to the ginger mixture and return to a simmer. The ginger stock should be just slightly thickened: add more cornflour liquid if necessary. Strain this dipping sauce and allow to cool to room temperature.

Divide the rocksalt between 4 plates and place 8 washed and dried oyster shells on each plate. On each shell put a small amount of pickled lettuce. Heat oil in a deep-fryer to 190°C. Dust the oysters with flour and dip in the beer batter. Fry oysters for about 15– 20 seconds only. Replace each oyster in a shell and serve with the ginger sauce.

YOUNG, FRESH SAUVIGNON BLANC. THE GRASSY TANG OF THE VARIETY AND THE CRISP ACID FINISH WILL ACT AS A COUNTERFOIL TO THE CREAMY TEXTURE OF THE OYSTERS, HEAT FROM THE CHILLI AND THE PIQUANCY OF THE GINGER.

3. WOOD-FIRE ROASTED PACIFIC OYSTERS WITH WASABI BUTTER & BRIOCHE CRUMBS

ingredients

250 g (8 oz) unsalted butter
2 teaspoons wasabi
24 oysters
½ loaf of brioche (p.160)
500 g (1 lb) rocksalt

method

Soften butter to room temperature. Add 2 teaspoons water to the wasabi to form a paste. Place unsalted butter and wasabi paste in a bowl and mix well.

Scrub the oysters to remove any dirt that may still be attached. Shuck the oysters, discard the lids and carefully remove any fragments of shell or grit that may litter the inside of the shell. Pour off most of the oyster juices into a small bowl and reserve for later use – to enhance something like a butter sauce for seafood.

Cut brioche into chunks and place in a food processor. Run motor until fine crumbs are created.

On an oven tray, spread the rocksalt and sit the oysters on the rocksalt. Place a small teaspoon of wasabi butter on each oyster. Have your wood-fired oven cranked up to about 400ºC (580ºF). If you don't have a wood-fired oven, turn your conventional oven to its maximum setting. Roast oysters for 3 minutes, remove from the oven and sprinkle them with a thin layer of brioche crumbs. Return to the oven and remove once the crumbs have toasted to a golden brown colour. Serve immediately.

STEELY DRY RIESLING. AN AROMATIC VARIETY SUCH AS RIESLING SUITS THIS DISH BEST AS THE FLORAL BOUQUET WILL BLEND SUPERBLY WITH THE WASABI. THE WINE MUST BE BONE-DRY TO MATCH THE OYSTERS, AS THE ACID IS NEEDED TO CUT THROUGH THEIR CREAMY TEXTURE.

4. STEAMED PINK-EYE CHAT POTATOES WITH CAVIARS & AN OYSTER SHOOTER

ingredients

16 pink-eye chat potatoes (or other variety with a waxy, buttery flesh, such as southern golds)
125 g (4 oz) crème fraiche
30 g (1 oz) sevruga caviar
30 g (1 oz) ocean trout roe
4 oysters
100 ml (3½ fl oz) premium vodka
100 ml (3½ fl oz) tomato juice
juice of ½ lemon
few drops of Tabasco sauce
few drops of Worcestershire sauce
freshly cracked black pepper

method

Pick out 16 potatoes of the same size, preferably a little smaller than a golf ball. Steam them until they are tender. While they are hot, cut a flat spot on each one to sit on to make them stable. With a small knife, cut the top off each potato and cut or scoop out a little extra flesh to make a small well.

In each of 4 shot glasses, place an oyster, some vodka, tomato juice, lemon juice, Tabasco and Worcestershire sauce. Crack some black pepper over each glass to finish.

Place 4 hot potatoes on each of 4 serving plates. With a teaspoon, place a small amount of crème fraiche in each well. Top with a small clump of caviar or roe. Each plate should have 2 sevruga potatoes and 2 ocean trout potatoes. The heat from the potatoes will melt the crème fraiche, so work quickly.

Place a shooter on each plate and serve. Using your fingers only, eat the caviar potatoes and then throw down the oyster shooter.

This is a good starter if you are expecting stiff guests. These caviar potatoes can also be used as a garnish for fish.

THE OYSTER SHOOTER IS THE SUGGESTION HERE, BUT AS AN ALTERNATIVE YOU MAY PREFER YOUR FAVOURITE SPARKLING WINE.

1. TUNA CARPACCIO ON SHAVED FENNEL WITH PRESERVED LEMON & SEVRUGA CAVIAR

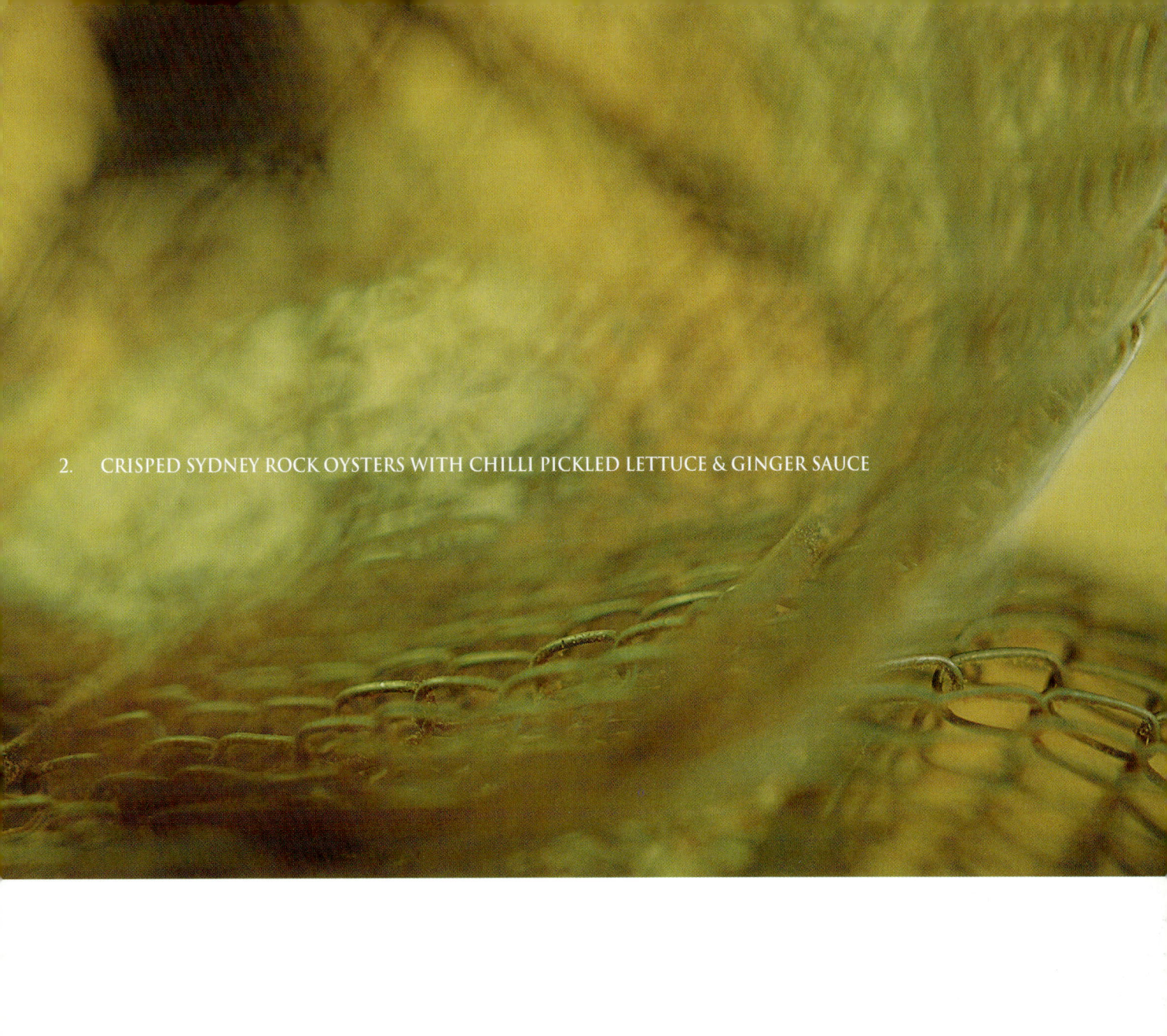
2. CRISPED SYDNEY ROCK OYSTERS WITH CHILLI PICKLED LETTUCE & GINGER SAUCE

5. ROAST SPRING BAY SCALLOPS WITH TOMATO & CUCUMBER SALSA

ingredients

½ continental cucumber
250 ml (8 fl oz) tomato concasse (p.163)
1 small Spanish onion, finely diced
1 bird's-eye chilli, minced
1 tablespoon chopped coriander
1 clove garlic, minced
200 ml (6½ fl oz) extra-virgin olive oil
juice of 2 limes
black pepper
24 scallops, on the half-shell

method

Peel the cucumber, cut in half lengthways and, using a teaspoon, remove the seeds. Dice the cucumber the same size as the tomato. The quantities of the 2 dices should be the same. Mix the tomato and cucumber in a bowl and add the onion, chilli and coriander.

In a separate bowl, mix the garlic and oil. Add half of this to the salsa and mix. Add lime juice and some freshly cracked black pepper.

Place scallops on their half-shells on an oven tray and drizzle with the remaining oil. Place in a wood-fired oven at 500°C (900°F). If you don't have a wood-fired oven, turn your conventional oven to its maximum setting. The scallops will sear very quickly on the outside and should only be just warm on the inside. The entire cooking time should only be about 2 minutes, depending upon the size of the scallops.

Remove scallops from the oven when ready, and spoon over the tomato and cucumber salsa.

FRUITY RIESLING WITH A MEDIUM-DRY FINISH. TOMATO ALWAYS PRESENTS PROBLEMS WHEN TRYING TO FIND THE IDEAL WINE MATCH. RIESLING WORKS BECAUSE ITS AROMATIC NOSE HAS ENOUGH NATURALLY VOLATILE FRAGRANCE NOT TO BE SWAMPED BY THE PUNGENCY OF THE TOMATO, ALTHOUGH THE STEELY GERMANIC STYLE DOES NOT MATCH WELL BECAUSE OF TOMATO'S HIGH ACID CONTENT.

6. CAESAR SALAD

ingredients

1 ficelle (small baguette)
2 tablespoons unsalted butter
1 clove garlic
12 thin slices kaiserfleisch
1 tablespoon brown sugar
2 cos lettuces
200 ml Caesar dressing (p.159)
16 anchovies
100 g (3½ oz) parmesan cheese
freshly ground black pepper, coarse

method

Cut 16 slices off the ficelle, each 5 mm (¼ in) thick. Very lightly, butter both sides of each slice and bake in a moderate oven (180°C/350°F) until golden brown. When cool, cut the garlic clove in half and rub each crouton with a cut surface of garlic.

Lay the kaiserfleisch slices on an oven tray and brush with a syrup made by dissolving 1 tablespoon brown sugar in 2 tablespoons water. Cook in a very hot oven (230°C/450°F) until crisp.

Clean cos of their darker outer leaves. Snap the younger light green leaves from the stem and wash in a sink of cold water. Dry using a salad spinner or shake well by hand. Place leaves in a large bowl and add the dressing. Mix very well. Divide leaves between 4 bowls or plates. Place an anchovy on each crouton and put 4 croutons on each salad. Arrange crisped kaiserfleisch on leaves also. Shave parmesan over and finish with pepper grinds.

THIS VERSION OF THE CLASSIC DISH HAS A DECEPTIVELY COMPLEX ARRAY OF FLAVOURS. SEMILLON THAT HAS BEEN BLENDED WITH A LITTLE SAUVIGNON BLANC, OR A STRAIGHT SEMILLON WITH A LIGHT TOUCH OF OAK MATURATION, ARE THE PREFERRED OPTIONS. IN BOTH STYLES, LOOK FOR A WINE WITH CRISP ACID TO BALANCE THE CREAMY, SMOOTH COATING OF THE DRESSING.

7. CHILLED ROASTED TOMATO SOUP WITH YABBIES & AVOCADO

ingredients

1 kg (2 lb) very ripe roma tomatoes
olive oil
1 medium onion, minced
2 cloves garlic, minced
2 teaspoons freshly ground cumin
1 teaspoon freshly ground coriander
1 tablespoon tomato paste
500 ml (16 fl oz) chicken stock (p.158)
50 ml (1½ fl oz) balsamic vinegar
salt and pepper
1 avocado, diced
8 yabbies, cooked and peeled
chervil

method

Lightly oil a baking tray and place tomatoes on it. Roast in oven on high heat (220°C/425°F), rotating occasionally. The tomatoes are ready when their skins begin to blister and bubble but are not too brown, about 15–20 minutes. Reserve roasting oil and juices from tomato.

In a saucepan, heat olive oil and add onion, garlic, cumin and coriander. Fry gently, without colouring items. When softened, add tomato paste and continue to cook. Add roasted tomatoes and chicken stock. Bring to the boil and simmer for 30 minutes. Purée and pass through a fine sieve. Adjust thickness to soup consistency with extra stock. Add balsamic vinegar, salt and pepper to flavour.

When cold, ladle into 4 bowls. Garnish with diced avocado and halved yabbie tails. Place sprigs of chervil on top. Drizzle reserved tomato juices around soup.

FRUITY RIESLING. LOOK FOR THE FULLY RIPE STYLES FROM THE WARMER REGIONS. THE WINE MUST HAVE POWERFUL FRUIT FLAVOURS TO STAND UP TO THE DEEP, RICH FLAVOUR OF THE TOMATO. WINES THAT HAVE A TRACE OF RESIDUAL SUGAR WOULD BE PREFERABLE, AS THE SWEETNESS COVERS THE ACIDITY IN THE DISH. FRUITY RIESLING HAS THE ADDED BONUS OF DRINKING WELL WHEN IT IS SERVED VERY COLD.

I AM A GREAT ADVOCATE OF WOOD-FIRED OVENS. IF YOU HAVE ENOUGH SPACE FOR A BARBECUE, THEN YOU HAVE ENOUGH SPACE FOR A SMALL OVEN. AND NOTHING BEATS THE AROMA OR FLAVOUR OF FOODS COOKED IN THIS MANNER. IT SHOULD NOT BE SEEN AS A FAD. IT IS A RETURN TO THE WAY COOKING STARTED. ALWAYS USE WOOD FROM FALLEN TREES.

8. CHILLED CAULIFLOWER SOUP WITH CURRY CREAM & SHUCKED OYSTERS

ingredients

24 oysters, unshucked
1 cauliflower
500 ml (16 fl oz) light chicken stock (p.158)
salt and pepper
2 teaspoons curry powder
2 tablespoons olive oil
125 ml (4 fl oz) crème fraiche

method

Using an oyster knife, open the oysters and place them, along with their juices, in a small bowl.

Trim cauliflower into small florets and cover with chicken stock. Bring to the boil and simmer until cauliflower is tender. Remove from heat and purée. Refrigerate, and season with salt and pepper when cold.

Fry the curry powder in olive oil for 1 minute without letting it smoke too much. Cool and add crème fraiche. Add some reserved oyster juices, a spoon at a time, to thin the curry cream to a spoonable consistency.

Ladle the soup into 4 shallow, wide soup plates. Dot each plate of soup with 6 little 'pools' of curry cream and place an oyster on each dot.

GRASSY SAUVIGNON BLANC, EITHER AS STRAIGHT VARIETAL OR BLENDED WITH SEMILLON. THE VEGETABLE-LIKE CHARACTERS OF THE WINE WORK WELL WITH ALL ELEMENTS OF THE DISH. IT WILL MATCH THE FLAVOUR OF THE CAULIFLOWER, COOL THE HEAT OF THE CURRY AND CUT THROUGH THE OYSTERS' CREAMY TEXTURE.

9. KING CRAB & BBQ PORK RICEPAPER ROLLS WITH TAMARIND SAUCE

ingredients

200 g (6½ oz) crabmeat, cooked and picked
200 g (6½ oz) bbq pork (char siu*), finely chopped
50 g (1½ oz) cooked rice vermicelli
½ carrot, julienned
¼ cucumber, seeded and julienned
50 g (1½ oz) beanshoots, chopped
2 spring onions, chopped
2 teaspoons chopped Thai basil
2 teaspoons chopped Vietnamese mint
2 tablespoons palm sugar
juice of 2 limes
2 tablespoons fish sauce
2 teaspoons freshly grated ginger
pinch of seasalt
12 ricepaper wrappers

tamarind dipping sauce
100 g (3½ oz) tamarind, in a block
100 ml (3½ fl oz) hoisin sauce
50 ml (1½ fl oz) Chinese rice wine
2 bird's-eye chillies, minced
75 g (2½ oz) palm sugar

*Barbecued pork, or *char siu*, can be bought from Chinese food stores. You often see it hanging in the window of such shops.

method

In a bowl combine crabmeat, pork, vermicelli, carrot, cucumber, beanshoots, spring onion, basil and mint.

In a small saucepan, dissolve the sugar in a little water over a low heat. Remove from heat and add the fish sauce, lime juice, ginger and seasalt. Cool and pour over the crab/pork mixture to taste. Keep any dressing not required for future use.

In a large, shallow bowl filled with lukewarm water, place the wrappers one at a time to soften. This should take about 30 seconds each. Remove from water and lie flat on a bench. Place 1 large tablespoon of filling in the centre of each, fold in the sides and roll up. Place on a plate or tray and cover with a damp cloth as you complete each one. Serve with tamarind dipping sauce.

To make dipping sauce, place the tamarind in a saucepan with 200 ml (6½ fl oz) of water and bring to the boil. Simmer for approximately 5 minutes, breaking up the block with a fork. Strain through a sieve to remove the seeds and add hoisin, rice wine and chillies. Dissolve the palm sugar in 75 ml (2½ fl oz) of water over low heat. Add to the tamarind mixture and cool.

A FRUITY RIESLING WITH RICHNESS IN THE MID PALATE AND A DRY FINISH. THE SWEET OPULENCE OF THE CRABMEAT REQUIRES RICHNESS IN THE WINE AND THE TAMARIND SAUCE MATCHES PERFECTLY WITH THE CITRUS FLAVOURS OF RIESLING. THE ACID AT THE FINISH IS A GREAT COUNTERFOIL TO THE GELATINOUS TEXTURE OF THE RICEPAPER.

10. TUNA TARTARE WITH EGGPLANT CRISPS & CORIANDER OIL

ingredients

150 ml (5 fl oz) olive oil
½ bunch coriander, chopped
2 large eggplants
250 ml (8 fl oz) vegetable oil
1 x 2.5 cm (1 in) knob ginger
400 g (13 oz) tuna, sashimi quality
2 small chillies, minced
1 teaspoon minced garlic
1 tablespoon minced Spanish onion
1 tablespoon tiny capers, chopped
4 teaspoons sesame oil
juice of 2 limes
black pepper

method

Place the olive oil and the chopped coriander bar 1 tablespoon into the workbowl of your food processor. Run for a couple of minutes and let stand for 2 hours. Strain and reserve the oil.

Using an electric slicer if you have one, or a mandolin, slice the eggplant very thinly. Put in a large bowl and sprinkle liberally with salt. Place on a cake rack on a tray for 15 minutes. This process will draw a lot of the water out of the eggplant and allow it to crisp up when fried. Rinse well under running water and pat dry.

Heat the vegetable oil and shallow-fry the eggplant until crisp and golden brown. Drain on paper towel. Slice the ginger very finely and also shallow-fry in the oil until crisp.

Cut tuna into 5 mm (¼ in) dice and put in a large bowl with the chilli, garlic, onion, capers and the reserved tablespoon of coriander. Cover and let sit in the refrigerator for 1 hour to allow the flavours to blend a little.

When ready to serve, remove tuna mixture from the refrigerator and add the sesame oil and lime juice. Season with freshly cracked black pepper. Place a piece of crisped eggplant on the centre of each serving plate. Spoon the mixture onto the eggplant and top with another eggplant crisp to create a 'sandwich'. Drizzle around coriander oil and garnish the top eggplant crisps with a few pieces of crisped ginger.

SAUVIGNON BLANC THAT IS FRUITY RATHER THAN GRASSY BUT HAS CRISP ACID AND A DRY FINISH. THE PASSIONFRUIT FRAGRANCE OF RIPE SAUVIGNON BLANC IS A GREAT PARTNER FOR THE AROMATICS OF THE CORIANDER, BUT THE WINE MUST BE DRY AND CRISP TO CUT AND LIFT THE FLESH OF THE FISH.

11. CHAR-GRILLED ASPARAGUS WITH CHOPPED EGG & PARMESAN OIL

ingredients

kept parmesan rinds
extra-virgin olive oil
32 asparagus spears, trimmed and peeled
4 eggs, hardboiled
parmesan shavings
freshly ground black pepper

method

Place parmesan rinds that have been kept from previously finished wedges of parmesan in a pot. Cover with extra-virgin olive oil and heat very gently. The temperature should never get above anything that you can't put your finger in. If the temperature gets too hot, the oil will break down and lose its fruitiness. Maintain this temperature for 15 minutes then remove from the heat. When cool, transfer oil and rinds into a sealable container that will not allow any light in. Allow oil 2–4 weeks to flavour.

Brush asparagus with a little oil and place on char-grill or a black iron griddle. Roll over to cook evenly. Remove and place 8 spears on each plate. Grate an egg on each plate of asparagus. Drizzle parmesan oil over each dish. Sprinkle with parmesan shavings and freshly ground black pepper.

SAUVIGNON BLANC, WITH ITS OFTEN-FOUND 'ASPARAGUS CHARACTER'. AN EASY MATCH. SEEK SAUVIGNON BLANCS FROM THE MARLBOROUGH REGION OF NEW ZEALAND IF YOU DESIRE AN OVERLOAD OF ASPARAGUS FLAVOUR.

11. CHAR-GRILLED ASPARAGUS WITH CHOPPED EGG & PARMESAN OIL

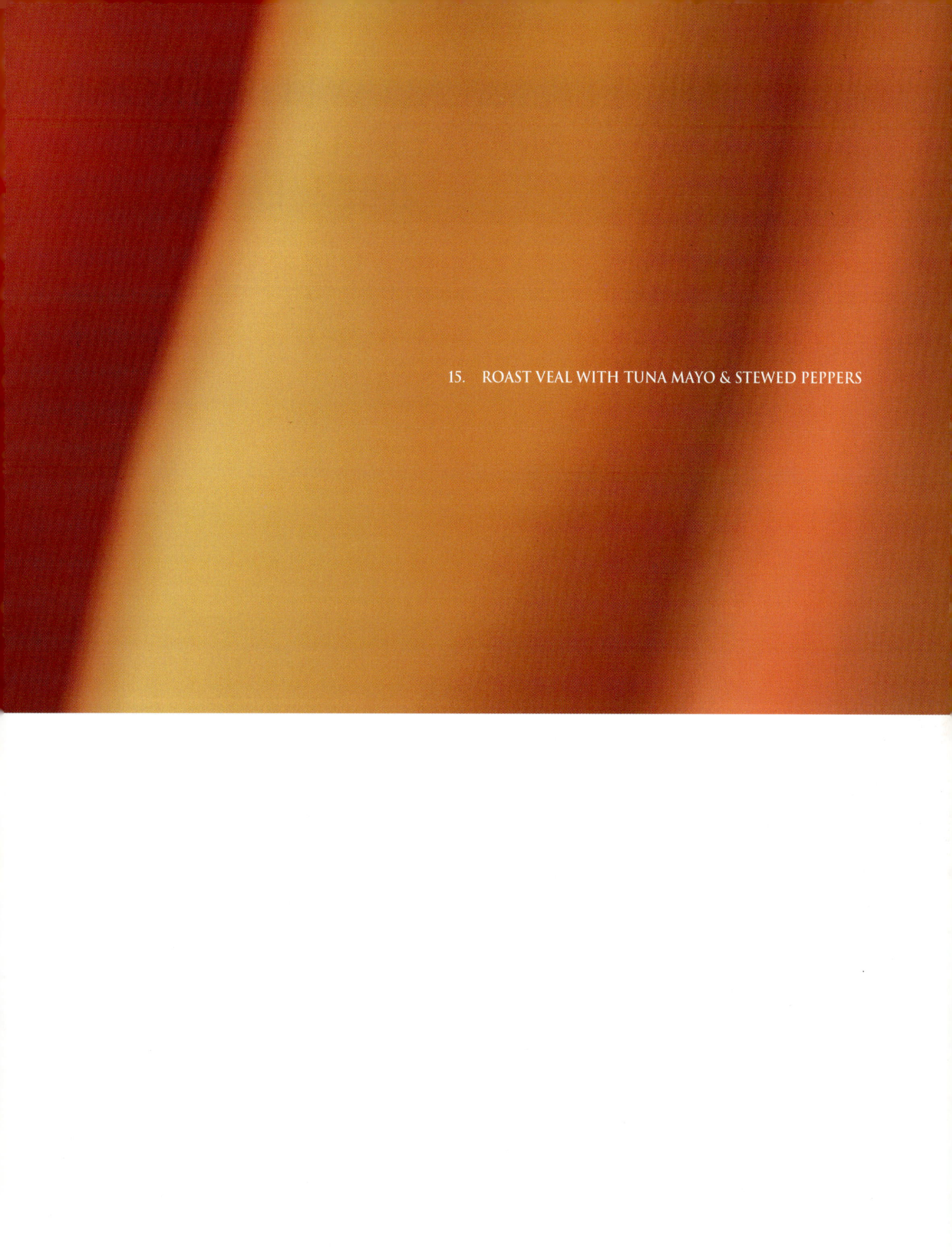

15. ROAST VEAL WITH TUNA MAYO & STEWED PEPPERS

12. LOBSTER SALAD WITH BROAD BEANS, SMOKED TOMATOES & BEET DRESSING

ingredients

2 tomatoes
1 rock lobster (about 800 g/1½ lb), cooked
1 medium beetroot
25 ml (¾ fl oz) red wine vinegar
75 g (2½ oz) podded broad beans
200 ml (6½ fl oz) extra-virgin olive oil
½ bunch chervil
freshly cracked black pepper

method

First remove the cores of the tomatoes and score the skins with a paring knife. Blanch in boiling water for 10 seconds to skin. Immerse in ice water and peel tomatoes when cool. Cut tomatoes in half and squeeze gently to remove seeds and excess juices.

It is not absolutely necessary to have a food smoker for this recipe as one can be made up from existing kitchen equipment. An old aluminium baking dish that is large enough to fit a cake rack is all you need. Soak your preferred wood chips in water for 30 minutes before placing on the bottom of smoking tray. Place cake rack over the wood chips. The item to be smoked (tomatoes in this recipe) should be placed on the rack and the whole tray covered with foil to create an airtight smoking chamber. This 'smoker' can then be placed directly over a stove top heat. The length of time required to smoke an item depends upon the item being smoked, and individual taste. The only rule is not to oversmoke anything as it will mask the natural flavours of the ingredient. The smoked tomatoes only take 5 minutes once the woodchips start to smoke. Allow tomatoes to cool in the smoker.

Remove meat from the tail of the lobster without damaging the flesh. The best way to do this is to use sharp poultry shears. Reserve all shell and legs to freeze for later use in a stock or bisque. Carefully cut lobster tails into medallions 5 mm (¼ in) thick.

Cut beetroot into quarters and put through a vegetable juicer. Place extracted beetroot juice in a saucepan and reduce by two-thirds. Cool and add red wine vinegar.

Cook broad beans in boiling salted water and refresh in ice water. Remove skins from the beans.

To serve, position a smoked tomato in the centre of each plate and surround with 4–5 medallions of lobster. Drizzle olive oil and beetroot vinegar around the outside of the medallions. Scatter broad beans over plate, garnish with sprigs of chervil and grind black pepper over.

PINOT GRIGIO, VERY RIPE AND FULL-BODIED. THIS IS A VERY DIFFICULT DISH TO MATCH AS IT HAS A MIXTURE OF CONTRASTING FLAVOURS. THE LOBSTER NEEDS A SMOOTH WINE WITH RICHNESS IN THE MID PALATE. THE BEETROOT NEEDS A WINE WITH A FRUIT FLAVOUR SIMILAR TO PINOT NOIR. PINOT GRIGIO MEETS THESE REQUIREMENTS.

13. GOAT'S CHEESE, FENNEL & OLIVE TART WITH RED PEPPER SAUCE

ingredients

1 quantity shortcrust pastry (p.161)
1 fennel bulb
50 g (1½ oz) unsalted butter
150 g (5 oz) mature goat's cheese
50 g (1½ oz) kalamata olives
1 teaspoon thyme
3 eggs
200 ml (6½ fl oz) cream
salt and pepper
1 large red pepper

method

Dust the bench lightly with flour and gently roll pastry out to line a 25 cm (10 in) tart ring. The pastry will be very delicate, so gently lift into the tart ring and, using your fingers, press into shape. Trim overhanging pastry. Refrigerate for 30 minutes.

Preheat oven to 170ºC (340ºF). Cover the pastry-lined tart ring with a sheet of baking paper and fill with pastry weights or rice that can be re-used as a pastry weight. Blind-bake for about 15 minutes until the pastry is light brown around the edges. Remove from oven and let cool.

Increase oven temperature to 190ºC (370ºF). Wash and trim the fennel bulb and cut into quarters. Remove centre stem and finely slice. Melt the butter in a pan and gently sweat the fennel for 10 minutes until softened. Remove from heat and cool. Spread the fennel over the bottom of the par-cooked pastry shell. Crumble the goat's cheese evenly over the fennel. Pit the olives and distribute evenly around the tart. Sprinkle the thyme leaves evenly. In a bowl, mix the eggs and cream, season with salt and pepper. Pour over the pie filling and bake in oven for 20 minutes or until filling is set and pastry golden brown.

To make the red pepper sauce, simply follow the method of blackening, peeling and puréeing the peppers explained in Red Pepper Terrine (p.26). If necessary, use a little stock or water to thin down slightly.

Serve the tart at room temperature or warmed with the red pepper sauce and a salad of small leaves.

SAUVIGNON BLANC THAT IS BOTH GRASSY AND FRUITY. THE FRESHNESS OF THE WINE LIFTS AND MOISTENS THE CHALKY TEXTURE OF THE GOAT'S CHEESE. THIS IS A NOTORIOUSLY DIFFICULT FOOD TO MATCH BUT SAUVIGNON BLANC IS THE IDEAL PARTNER. THE FRUITY CHARACTERS WILL SUIT THE CHEESE WHILST THE GRASSY CHARACTER WILL MATCH ALL THE VEGETABLE FLAVOURS IN THE DISH.

14. RED PEPPER TERRINE WITH A MUSSEL & WATERCRESS SALAD

ingredients

100 g (3½ oz) green lentils
4 red peppers
6 leaves gelatine
250 ml (8 fl oz) chicken stock
150 ml (5 fl oz) white wine
24 mussels
2 shallots
1 tomato
1 bunch watercress
50 ml (1½ fl oz) extra-virgin olive oil
3 teaspoons balsamic vinegar
freshly cracked black pepper

GRASSY SAUVIGNON BLANC. THIS DISH HAS STRONG VEGETABLE AND HERBAL FLAVOURS WHICH DEMAND A SAUVIGNON BLANC THAT IS GRASSY AND HERBACEOUS. THE CRISP ACID AT THE FINISH WILL ADD A LOVELY CONTRAST TO THE CRUNCHY TEXTURE OF THE TOAST.

method

Wash the lentils and soak in cold water overnight.

Core the red peppers, and cut into sections so that they can be laid flat on an oven tray, skin side up. Place under a very hot grill close to the heat source to blacken the skins. When blackened, remove and cover with a tea towel for 5 minutes. Peel the skins and purée the flesh in a blender (a food processor will not purée the peppers fine enough).

This recipe requires 500 ml (16 fl oz) of red pepper purée. It may be necessary to do more peppers in order to yield sufficient purée.

Soak the leaf gelatine in cold water for about 3 minutes to soften. Add the gelatine to the chicken stock and heat to dissolve. Add to the red pepper purée, mix in well, and pour into a small terrine mould to set.

Bring the white wine to the boil in a wide pan. Add the mussels and cover with a lid. Steam until all mussels open, stirring occasionally to mix up. When mussels have opened, strain the cooking liquor into a saucepan and reduce by half. Reserve.

Rinse the lentils and cover with fresh water. Bring to the boil and simmer until tender. Refresh under cold water immediately.

Finely slice shallots into small rings and shallow-fry until golden and crispy.

Score the skin of the tomato and immerse in boiling water until the skin starts to lift. Cool in ice water and peel. Cut in half and remove the seeds and water. Cut into 1-cm (½-in) dice.

Wash and pick the watercress to remove any tough stalks.

In a bowl, mix the mussels, lentils, shallots and tomato dice. Add 1 tablespoon of the reserved mussel stock along with the extra-virgin olive oil and balsamic vinegar. Toss well and add a little freshly cracked black pepper.

With a warm, sharp knife cut the terrine into 1 cm (½ in) thick slices. Place a slice on each serving plate, drizzle with a little of your best extra-virgin olive oil and spoon a small amount of mussel salad alongside. Serve with toasted basil bread (p.160).

15. ROAST VEAL WITH TUNA MAYO & STEWED PEPPERS

ingredients

1 carrot
1 small onion
1 stick celery
2 cloves garlic
olive oil
4 anchovies
1 tablespoon large capers
1 x 180 g (6½ oz) can tuna
3 tablespoons red wine vinegar
250 ml (8 fl oz) thick mayonnaise
salt and pepper
1 veal nut, about 800 g–1 kg (1½–2 lb)
1 red pepper
1 yellow pepper
1 green pepper
1 small bunch chives, finely chopped
2 tablespoons small capers

method

Preheat oven to 200°C (400°F). Chop onion, carrot and celery into medium dice. Place in a pan or roasting tray along with the garlic and 2 tablespoons olive oil. Roast in oven for about 20–30 minutes, tossing periodically. Cool.

Place roast vegetables in a food processor with anchovies, large capers, tuna and red wine vinegar. Process until smooth. Add to mayonnaise, mix well and season to taste.

Increase oven temperature to 220°C (440°F). Season veal nut and roast for 15 minutes, then reduce heat to 200°C for a further 10 minutes. The veal should be medium-rare – cooking times will vary according to the size of the nut so adjust the timing.

Peel peppers and cut into 5-mm (¼-in) dice. Place in a frying pan with 125 ml (4 fl oz) olive oil and stew very slowly until tender. Drain and reserve the oil. Heat the reserved oil and fry the small capers until crisp.

Slice the veal across the grain very thinly (2 mm/⅛ in). Lay out on the plates in the manner of a carpaccio and smatter the tuna mayo across it. Sprinkle over stewed pepper, chopped chives and fried capers. Season liberally with freshly ground black pepper.

FRESH, UNWOODED CHARDONNAY. THE STONEFRUIT CHARACTER OF UNADULTERATED CHARDONNAY WILL HIGHLIGHT THE SUCCULENT, NUTTY FLAVOUR OF THE VEAL. THE WINE SHOULD BE CRISP WITH ACID TO CUT THROUGH THE RICHNESS OF THE MAYONNAISE.

16. SMOKED SALMON STACK WITH PICKLED CUCUMBER, HORSERADISH & LATTICE CHIPS

18. BBQ KING PRAWNS WITH EGGPLANT–HALOUMI FRITTERS, TABOULEH & TURMERIC OIL

16. SMOKED SALMON STACK WITH PICKLED CUCUMBER, HORSERADISH & LATTICE CHIPS

ingredients

1 large potato
500 ml (16 fl oz) vegetable oil
150 ml (5 fl oz) crème fraiche
2 tablespoons freshly grated horseradish
½ continental cucumber
2 tablespoons salt
50 ml (1½ fl oz) white wine vinegar
1 teaspoon castor sugar
50 g (1½ oz) rocket
12 slices smoked salmon

method

Peel the potato. Slice on a mandolin with the crinkle cut blade. Turn the potato 90° between each slice. Adjust the blade so that each slice is perforated or 'latticed'. Heat the vegetable oil in a saucepan and fry the lattice potatoes until golden brown.

Combine horseradish and crème fraiche in a bowl and reserve.

Peel and seed the cucumber after cutting in half lengthways. Shave the cucumber into long strips with a vegetable peeler or slicer. Salt and place on a wire rack for 15 minutes. Wash off salt and pat dry. Place wilted cucumber in a bowl with vinegar and sugar. Leave for 15 minutes.

To construct the dish, place 1 lattice chip on the centre of each plate. Then place in order: a layer of rocket, 1½ slices of salmon, a layer of pickled cucumber, a layer of horseradish cream, then another lattice chip, and follow the same sequence to finish with a lattice chip.

MEDIUM-BODIED BUT CREAMY-TEXTURED CHARDONNAY. LOOK FOR A CHARDONNAY WITH A FAIR PROPORTION OF MALOLACTIC FERMENTATION. THIS WILL GIVE THE WINE A CREAMY TEXTURE WHICH WILL MATCH THE DEPTH OF FLAVOUR OF THE SALMON. THE WINE SHOULD BE SOFT AT THE FINISH AS THERE IS AMPLE SHARPNESS AT THE FINISH OF THE DISH DUE TO THE PICKLED CUCUMBERS.

17. OCEAN TROUT GRAVLAX WITH GRILLED CORNCAKES & SNOWPEA FOLIAGE

ingredients

1 fillet ocean trout, about 800 g (1½ lb)
500 g (1 lb) rocksalt
440 g (14 oz) sugar
6 tablespoons chopped dill
2 tablespoons white peppercorns, crushed
2 corn cobs
1 small Spanish onion
3 tablespoons chopped coriander
1 clove garlic, minced
1 bird's-eye chilli, minced
1 egg
100 ml (3½ fl oz) cream
25 g (¾ oz) flour
2 egg yolks
100 ml (3½ fl oz) white wine vinegar
200 ml (6½ fl oz) olive oil
50 g (1½ oz) snowpea foliage
1 roasted red pepper (p.164), diced
2 tablespoons chopped chives

method

Remove all bones from trout fillet with tweezers or pointy-nosed pliers. Mix rocksalt and sugar together in a bowl. Add dill and peppercorns. Spread half of this mixture on a small tray and place ocean trout fillet on top, skin side up. Spread remaining mixture over the skin of the fish and place another tray over the whole thing. Weigh down top tray with a few jam jars or such like. The fish should be removed from curing mixture after 6–8 hours, depending upon the size of the fillet – the larger the fish the longer it will take to cure. When ready, wash fillet quickly under water, pat dry and wrap in plastic film and refrigerate.

Cook corn cobs in boiling salted water for 5 minutes. Remove from water and cut kernels from cobs. Place kernels in a bowl and add onion, coriander, garlic, chilli, egg, cream and flour. Mix well and season with salt and pepper. Spoon into a hot, lightly oiled pan to a diameter of 10 cm (4 in) – mixture will make at least 4 corncakes. When golden brown on the underside, flip with a spatula and brown on the reverse side. Remove carefully and reserve.

Place egg yolks and vinegar in food processor and turn motor on. In a steady stream add the olive oil. Season mayonnaise.

Cut roasted peppers into 5-mm (¼-in) dice. Spread a small amount of dressing over the base of each plate to its perimeter. Place a corncake on the centre of each plate and top with a few pieces of snowpea foliage. Remove gravlax from plastic wrap, slice as fine as possible on a 30° angle from the horizontal and drape over the foliage. Sprinkle diced peppers and chives in dressing, and grind some black pepper over the whole ensemble.

FRESH, FRUITY UNWOODED CHARDONNAY. THE STONEFRUIT FLAVOUR OF CHARDONNAY WILL SUIT THE RICH OCEAN TROUT FLAVOUR, AND THE CRISP FINISH TO WINES OF THIS STYLE WILL CUT THROUGH BOTH THE CORNCAKES AND THE OILY TEXTURE OF THE OCEAN TROUT.

18. BBQ KING PRAWNS WITH EGGPLANT-HALOUMI FRITTERS, TABOULEH & TURMERIC OIL

ingredients

200 ml (6½ fl oz) olive oil
2 tablespoons turmeric
16 green king prawns
1 Lebanese eggplant
100 g (3½ oz) haloumi cheese
100 g (3½ oz) self-raising flour
2 tablespoons cornflour
375 ml (12 fl oz) Cooper's Pale Ale
1 bunch flat leaf parsley
½ bunch watercress, chopped
3 tablespoons cracked wheat
125 ml (4 fl oz) tomato concasse (p.163)
1 clove garlic, minced
extra-virgin olive oil
juice of 1 lemon

method

Place 4 tablespoons of olive oil in a small pan. Add the turmeric and fry to release a pungent aroma. Take off the heat and add the remaining oil. Return to the heat and very gently heat for 15 minutes without oil ever getting too hot to touch. Store in an airtight container for one week before using. Shake vigorously for 20 seconds each day.

Shell the prawns, removing the head as well. Cut along the back to butterfly and remove any entrails in the process. Put aside. Slice eggplant on a 45° angle to create 8 thin, oval slices. Lightly sprinkle with salt and place over a cake rack to drain liquids for about 20 minutes. Wash eggplant slices and pat dry.

Slice haloumi cheese finely and make 4 'sandwiches' by placing the cheese between slices of eggplant. Cover with a damp cloth and put aside.

To make the batter, combine the flours in a bowl and whisk in the beer until liquid is smooth and even.

Blanch parsley in boiling water for 15 seconds and place in a blender with the absolute minimum of water it takes to purée the parsley. Purée and strain through a super-fine sieve or muslin cloth (only a couple of tablespoons of juice will be yielded).

To make tabouleh, combine the watercress, cracked wheat, tomato, garlic, extra-virgin oil and lemon juice in a bowl and toss well. Season.

Quickly barbecue prawns, or sear in a smear of oil in a heavy frypan. Lightly dust the eggplant sandwiches with flour, dip in batter and fry until golden brown. Halve the eggplant sandwiches. Place a spoonful of tabouleh on the centre of each plate and top with 2 pieces of eggplant fritter. Surround with 4 barbecued prawns each and the dish can be finished off with a drizzle of turmeric oil and parsley juice.

FRUITY RIESLING WITH A DRY FINISH. THE AROMATIC ELEMENTS OF THE WINE WILL COOL THE HEAT OF THE CURRY OIL WHILST THE CITRUS FLAVOUR TYPICAL OF RIESLING WILL HIGHLIGHT THE SWEET FLESH OF THE PRAWNS.

WHENEVER YOU CAN, PURCHASE CRUSTACEANS LIVE. TOO MUCH IS LEFT TO CHANCE IN BUYING THEM ANY OTHER WAY. AS LONG AS THEY'RE KICKING, YOU KNOW THEY ARE FRESH. BUT TREAT THEM HUMANELY. IMMERSE THEM IN A SINK OF ICED WATER FOR 30 MINUTES TO SLOW DOWN THEIR METABOLISM BEFORE COOKING. THEN THEY WON'T FEEL A THING.

19. YABBIE SALAD WITH GAZPACHO SAUCE & GALETTE POTATO

ingredients

1 kg (2 lb) live yabbies
½ green pepper
½ red pepper
¼ continental cucumber
2 cloves garlic
½ Spanish onion
2 ripe tomatoes
50 ml (1½ fl oz) red wine vinegar
salt and freshly ground black pepper
2 small to medium potatoes
100 ml (3½ fl oz) clarified butter
salt and freshly ground black pepper
100 g (3½ oz) mesclun
extra-virgin olive oil
salmon roe for garnish

FRUITY RIESLING WITH A TRACE OF SWEETNESS AT THE FINISH. THE CITRUS FLAVOUR OF THE RIESLING IS A SUPERB MATCH FOR THE YABBIES - AND CRUSTACEANS IN GENERAL. THE DOMINANT TOMATO FLAVOUR REQUIRES THAT THE WINE SHOULD HAVE A LITTLE RESIDUAL SUGAR AT THE BACK OF THE PALATE.

method

Cook yabbies in a pot of boiling salted water for 4 minutes. Do not refresh but allow them to cool to room temperature. When cool, remove the heads and peel the tails, keeping the tailmeat in one piece.

Roughly chop the peppers, cucumber, garlic, onion and tomato and place in the workbowl of a food processor with the vinegar. Run the motor for 10 seconds. Stop motor and scrape down the sides of the workbowl with a spatula. Run again for a further 10 seconds or until the resulting sauce is of an even texture with fine pieces of the ingredients still visible. Season to taste.

Preheat oven to 180°C (350°F). Peel the potatoes and trim into cylinders of 3 cm (1¼ in) diameter. Slice into 1-mm (¹⁄₁₆-in) thick discs using an electric slicer or mandolin. Pat the potato discs with paper towel to absorb any excess water and place in a bowl. Pour over warm clarified butter and toss to coat potato discs. Season lightly. On a non-stick baking sheet, arrange the discs in a slightly overlapping fashion so that about 20 discs will create a 6-cm (2½-in) circle. Repeat this process to create 4 circles. Brush each 'raw galette' with a little more clarified butter and bake in oven. When the underside is golden brown, turn the galettes over and cook until evenly golden and crisp: about 5-6 minutes per side.

Cover the bottom of each of 4 serving plates with a thin film of gazpacho sauce. Place a 6-cm (2½-in) pastry cutter or ring on the centre of one of the plates. Pack some mesclun that has been lightly dressed with extra-virgin olive oil and red wine vinegar into the ring and top with 5–8 yabbie tails, depending upon their size. Carefully lift the cutter off the plate so as not to upset the arrangement. Place a galette potato on the yabbies and top with a small spoon of salmon roe. Drizzle some extra-virgin olive oil around in the gazpacho sauce.

20. TWICE-BAKED ROAST GARLIC SOUFFLÉ WITH PARSLEY SAUCE & SAUTÉD SNAILS

ingredients

1 head garlic
25 g (1 oz) unsalted butter
25 g (1 oz) flour
50 ml (1½ fl oz) milk
2 egg yolks
6 egg whites
salt
1 bunch flat leaf parsley
100 ml (3½ fl oz) chicken stock (p.158)
100 ml (3½ fl oz) cream
24 fresh garden snails, cooked*
unsalted butter

*Most suppliers of fresh snails will have already cooked them, so they only require a light sautéing at the end of the preparation. It is best not to use anything but the fresh product – avoid tinned snails at all cost.

method

Preheat oven to 200°C (400°F). Place the whole head of garlic in a hot oven to bake until tender (about 20 minutes). Whilst the garlic is baking, melt the butter in a small saucepan, stir in the flour, and cook roux for about 1 minute. Heat milk to just boiling point and add to roux a little at a time, mixing properly between additions until a thick and smooth sauce has been formed. Remove from the heat, cool slightly, and add the yolks one at a time, again mixing properly between additions.

Cut the head of garlic in half across the middle and squeeze out the pulp or remove it with a pointed knife. Give it a quick mash before adding to the white sauce.

Reduce oven temperature to 170°C (340°F). In a copper bowl, whisk the egg whites with 2 pinches of salt until they hold firm, stiff peaks. (It is important to use a copper bowl as it prevents the protein breaking out of the egg whites – this appears as little white flecks and does not assist good soufflé making.) Gently fold the hot garlicky mixture into the egg white until evenly incorporated. Spoon into dariole moulds that have been well buttered, put moulds in a waterbath and bake for 20 minutes. When cool, remove soufflés from their moulds very carefully as they will be extremely fragile. (The recipe to this stage can be done several hours ahead.)

Heat the chicken stock and add the parsley until it wilts. Purée in a blender and when perfectly smooth pour into a small saucepan. Add the cream and bring to the boil. Season lightly.

Preheat oven to 190°C (380°F). Pour the sauce into 4 shallow cocotte dishes to a depth of about 3–4 mm (⅛ in). On each pool of sauce, place a soufflé and bake in oven until the soufflés 'blow' back up to their full glory, about 8–10 minutes. Two minutes before they are ready, quickly sauté the snails in a little unsalted butter and lightly season. Remove the cocotte dishes from the oven and arrange the snails around each soufflé.

NUTTY FULL-BODIED CHARDONNAY. THE DEEP PUNGENCY OF GARLIC COMBINED WITH THE AROMATIC HERBAL CHARACTER OF PARSLEY CALLS FOR A RICH WINE WITH DEPTH OF FLAVOUR IN THE MID PALATE. RICH BARREL-FERMENTED CHARDONNAY IS THE BEST OPTION.

21. BBQ SALMON NICOISE SALAD

ingredients

4 x 130 g (4 oz) salmon steaks
18 cherry tomatoes
200 g (6½ oz) baby green beans
8 quail eggs
4 pink-eye chat potatoes
1 small Spanish onion
18 kalamata olives
4 anchovies
100 ml (3½ fl oz) extra-virgin olive oil
1 tablespoon balsamic vinegar
100 ml (3½ fl oz) Caesar dressing (p.159), slightly thinned for drizzling
2 tablespoons chopped chives
freshly ground black pepper

FRUITY UNWOODED CHARDONNAY. THE PEACH AND MELON FLAVOURS OF RIPE CHARDONNAY FRUIT BLENDS WITH THE SUCCULENT, SMOOTH-TEXTURED FLESH OF THE SALMON. THE FRUITY CHARACTER SOFTENS THE SLIGHT BITTERNESS FROM BARBECUING AND BALANCES THE ACID FINISH OF THE DRESSING.

method

Firstly, cut cherry tomatoes in half, place on an oven tray cut side up, and put in an oven no hotter than 80°C (170°F). This will semi-dry the tomatoes without colouring them, and in doing so will intensify their flavour. Remove from oven.

Cook beans in lightly salted water and refresh in cold water. Dry and put aside. Place quail eggs in a small saucepan, cover with water and bring to a boil. Simmer for 3 minutes and refresh under cold running water. Cook potatoes whole in simmering water until tender. Remove and refresh. Pat dry, slice and reserve. Peel onion and finely slice, separating the layers in the process. Pit the olives and cut in half. Cut the anchovies into julienne (if you find the flavour of anchovies a little strong, they can be soaked in milk for 10–15 minutes to tone down).

In a large bowl, place the semi-dried tomatoes, beans, peeled and halved quail eggs, sliced potatoes, onion, olives and anchovies. Add the olive oil and balsamic vinegar and toss as gently as possible to avoid damaging any of the ingredients.

This recipe recommends that the salmon be barbecued, but it may be pan-seared if a barbecue is unavailable or inconvenient. Whatever the method, remove the salmon from refrigeration and bring it up to room temperature. The fish should be seared quickly, and removed from the heat when cooked no more than medium-rare.

Divide salad between serving plates. Cut each piece of fish into about 6 pieces and arrange over salad. Drizzle over a little thinned Caesar dressing, sprinkle with chopped chives and grind over some black pepper.

This dish can also be served from one large platter as part of an alfresco spread.

22. MARINATED YOUNG LEEKS WITH CRAB REMOULADE

ingredients

16 young leeks
100 ml (3½ fl oz) white wine vinegar
1 teaspoon black peppercorns
2 bay leaves
2 cloves garlic
few strands saffron
4 sprigs thyme
250 ml (8 fl oz) extra-virgin olive oil
200 ml (7 fl oz) mayonnaise (p.159)
1 dill pickle, finely chopped
1 teaspoon capers, finely chopped
2 anchovies, chopped
1 tablespoon chopped flat leaf parsley
1 egg, hardboiled and chopped
200 g (6½ oz) fresh crabmeat, cooked and picked
125 ml (4 fl oz) tomato concasse (p.163)

method

Trim the leeks of their roots. Cut off the top 4–5 cm (2–3 in) to get rid of the darker green, tougher leaves. Wash gently in a bath of cold water to dislodge any dirt that may have accumulated between layers.

In a non-corrosive saucepan, combine the vinegar, peppercorns, bay leaves, garlic, saffron and thyme and bring to the boil. Allow to cool slowly to room temperature and add to the extra-virgin olive oil.

Bring a large saucepan of lightly salted water to the boil. Gently immerse the leeks and simmer until they are cooked but firm. Remove from the water and dry completely before laying them down in a single layer in a plastic or stainless steel tray. Pour over the vinegar/olive oil marinade and refrigerate for 4 hours, rolling the leeks hourly.

In a bowl, combine the mayonnaise, dill pickles, capers, anchovies, parsley, egg, crab and tomato. Mix well and season with freshly cracked black pepper (salt will not be necessary due to the saltiness of the anchovies). The mayonnaise should do no more than just bind the other ingredients.

Drain the leeks of their marinade and lay out on serving plates. Spoon the crab remoulade across the centre of the leeks.

YOUTHFUL SEMILLON. THE FRESH STRAW AND SUBTLE GRASSY CHARACTER IN YOUNG SEMILLON MATCHES WELL WITH THE EQUALLY SUBTLE FLAVOUR OF LEEK, AND THE CRISP ACID AT THE FINISH WILL GIVE A LIFT TO THE RICH TEXTURE OF THE REMOULADE.

19. YABBIE SALAD WITH GAZPACHO SAUCE & GALETTE POTATO

21. BBQ SALMON NICOISE SALAD

23. GRATINEE OF YOUNG ARTICHOKES WITH MUD CRAB & TOMATO SALSA

ingredients

375 ml (12 fl oz) tomato concasse (p.163)
1 small Spanish onion, finely diced
1 clove garlic, minced
1 bird's-eye chilli, minced
2 tablespoons chopped coriander
200 ml (6½ fl oz) extra-virgin olive oil
juice of 2 limes
salt and freshly ground black pepper
6 young artichokes
200 g (6½ oz) crabmeat, cooked and picked
100 ml (3½ fl oz) extra-virgin olive oil
1 tablespoon unsalted butter
60 g (2 oz) brioche crumbs or fresh breadcrumbs
2 teaspoons freshly grated horseradish

UNWOODED CHARDONNAY WITH AN ABUNDANCE OF FRUIT AND A SOFT FINISH. ARTICHOKES CAN MAKE WINE TASTE METALLIC SO IT IS DESIRABLE TO CHOOSE A RIPE, FRUITY WINE. ENSURE THAT THE WINE IS NOT SHARP WITH ACID AT THE FINISH AS THIS WOULD CLASH WITH THE ACIDITY OF THE TOMATO.

method

Place tomato in a bowl with the onion, garlic, chilli, coriander, 200 ml (6½ fl oz) oil and lime juice. Mix well and season to taste with salt and pepper.

Put a saucepan of water on to boil and lightly salt. Cut a lemon in half and add to the water. Trim the artichokes of all the tough outer leaves. Cut off the stems 5 cm (2 in) below the base of the heads. Lightly scrape the stems with a vegetable peeler. Cut off the tops of the artichokes to about 5 cm (2 in) of the stem to lose the tough tips of the leaves. Once the artichokes are trimmed down to this point, quickly immerse in the boiling water. Simmer and cook until artichokes are tender, about 25 minutes. Remove from water and refresh in iced water. Dry off and cut each artichoke in half lengthways. Remove and discard 'furry' choke from the centre of each artichoke if there is any. A little more 'good' artichoke may have to be removed to form a cavity for the crab – reserve this to garnish a salad or soup.

Place the crabmeat in a bowl and season with a little salt and pepper. Add a drizzle of extra-virgin olive oil and gently toss. Divide between the 12 halves of artichoke, filling each cavity generously.

Melt the unsalted butter in a frypan and when bubbling add the brioche crumbs and grated horseradish. Toss until crumbs are golden brown and crispy.

Preheat oven to 180°C (350°F). Place the artichokes on a lightly oiled baking tray. Bake for 5 minutes, sprinkle crumb mixture liberally over each artichoke and continue to heat for another 3 minutes. Remove from the oven.

Divide tomato salsa between 4 plates and place 3 halves of artichoke on each.

24. SEARED SARDINE FILLETS WITH TOMATO-FENNEL STEW & GREEN OLIVE TAPENADE

ingredients

3 ripe tomatoes
2 tablespoons extra-virgin olive oil
1 small onion, sliced
2 cloves garlic, minced
2 fennel bulbs, sliced
12 oregano leaves
155 g (5 oz) green olives
4 anchovy fillets
1 tablespoon capers
extra 1 clove garlic
16 sardines
olive oil

method

With a sharp paring knife, remove the eye and score the top of each tomato. Immerse in boiling water for 10 seconds or until the skin starts to blister. Place in iced water to cool. Peel the tomatoes and cut in half. Gently squeeze each tomato half to remove all the seeds and water. Place on a lightly oiled tray, cut side up, in an oven on the lowest temperature possible for about 30 minutes. This will slowly remove all remaining liquid and intensify the flavour of the tomato. Be careful that the heat is very low in the oven as we want to keep the redness of the tomatoes and not cause any browning.

While the tomatoes are in the oven, put the extra-virgin olive oil in a heavy frypan over a very low heat (if the heat is too high, the olive oil will break down and lose its fruitiness). Add the onion and garlic and stir, maintaining a very low heat. After 2 minutes, add the fennel and continue to cook very slowly.

Remove the tomatoes from the oven and chop roughly on a board. Add to the fennel mixture along with the oregano. Continue to cook on a very low heat for a further 15 minutes, adding more olive oil if necessary.

On a chopping board, bash the green olives with a rolling pin or meat cleaver to flatten and expose the stone. Remove the stones and add anchovies, capers and remaining garlic clove to the olives. With a large knife, chop the ingredients together until they are quite fine but still textured. Transfer to a non-corrosive bowl and add extra-virgin olive oil to form a coarse paste.

Remove the heads from the sardines. Remove the backbone from each fish by making an incision along both sides of the backbone, the full length of each fish. Using your fingers, carefully take out the backbone and as many of the fine ribs as possible.

Dust each fillet with a little flour and sear in plain olive oil over high heat for no more than 15 seconds each side.

Spoon the tomato–fennel stew on to the centre of each plate and arrange 4 sardine fillets over each pile. Top with green olive tapenade.

FRUITY AND SLIGHTLY SWEET RIESLING. THE SWEET FINISH IS IMPORTANT IN MATCHING THE TOMATO WHILST THE CITRUS FRUIT FLAVOUR WILL NOT BE OVERPOWERED BY THE STRONG FLAVOUR OF THE FISH.

25. PUMPKIN TORTELLINI WITH MUSTARD FRUITS & CITRUS BUTTER

ingredients

1 quantity pasta dough
   (p.161)
1 egg, beaten
shaved parmesan
chopped mustard fruits

filling
1 small pumpkin, baked and
   roughly mashed to yield
   250 ml (8 fl oz) pulp
60 g (2 oz) ricotta
60 g (2 oz) parmesan, grated
2 tablespoons chopped
   mustard fruits
1 egg, lightly beaten
salt and freshly ground
   black pepper

sauce
juice of 2 lemons
60 ml (2 fl oz) chicken stock
   (p.158)
125 g (4 oz) unsalted butter

MATURE SEMILLON WITH HONEYED CHARACTERS. THE TOASTED HONEY EVIDENT IN A MATURE SEMILLON IS SUPERB FOR THIS DISH AS IT WILL HIGHLIGHT THE SWEETNESS OF THE PUMPKIN AND ALSO BLEND WITH THE TANG OF THE MUSTARD FRUITS.

method

Combine pumpkin in a bowl with ricotta, parmesan, mustard fruits and egg. Mix well. Season with a little salt and freshly ground black pepper. Put aside.

Set up pasta machine on a bench. Divide dough into 3. Roll each batch through the pasta machine, starting on the thickest setting and working the dough gradually to the thinnest setting. Cover each batch with plastic wrap before proceeding to the next one. When all sheets have been rolled, take one and cut into squares about 5 cm (2 in) per side. Place a teaspoon of filling in the centre of each square, and brush two edges of each square with beaten egg, in an 'L' shape. Bring two opposing corners together and seal to enclose filling in a triangular pasta shape. Wrap each triangle around your little finger to join the 2 ends of the longest side together. Press these together. Repeat process with remaining 2 pasta sheets.

Cook tortellini in gently rolling boiling water for 2 minutes. Remove and place in a wide saucepan with lemon juice and chicken stock. Heat, gently rotating pan to avoid sticking. When liquid is hot, add butter a tablespoon at a time until fully incorporated. Do not boil this sauce as it may easily separate. Salt lightly to taste.

Spoon tortellini on to plates and garnish with chopped mustard fruits, parmesan shavings and cracked black pepper.

26. ASPARAGUS & FONTINA TORTELLI WITH VEGETABLE ESSENCE & TRUFFLE OIL

ingredients

1 quantity pasta dough (p.161)
1 egg, lightly beaten
1 tablespoon white truffle oil

filling
200 g (6½ oz) asparagus
100 g (3½ oz) ricotta
100 g (3½ oz) fontina
salt and freshly ground black pepper

essence
1 leek
1 carrot
1 onion
1 stick celery
1 tomato
2 cloves garlic
2 sprigs thyme
1 teaspoon white peppercorns

method

Dice leek, carrot, onion, celery, tomato and garlic. Place in a saucepan with thyme, peppercorns and 1 litre (1¾ pints) water. Bring to the boil and simmer for 1 hour. Strain and return to the heat. Reduce until only 300 ml of stock is left: an essence.

Prepare asparagus by lightly peeling and removing the tough part of the stem. Cut into 2-cm (¾-in) sections and cook in lightly salted boiling water until tender. Remove and cool in iced water. Take the asparagus tips and put them aside as a garnish. Place the remaining asparagus in a food processor and pulse a few times to create a not-too-fine mince. Mix in a bowl with the ricotta and fontina and season with salt and freshly ground black pepper.

Set up a pasta machine on a bench. Lightly dust the bench with flour before starting to avoid the dough sticking. Work the dough through the rollers starting on the thickest setting and gradually reducing the settings until the desired thickness has been achieved. When all the dough has been rolled out to create thin sheets, use a ring cutter to cut circles of approximately 6 cm (2½ in) diameter. Pipe or spoon out asparagus mixture on to the centre of each circle. Brush the outside of the circles with a little beaten egg and fold to create half moon shapes.

Cook tortelli in simmering water. Heat up the vegetable essence and ladle into wide bowls to a depth of 5 mm (¼ in). With a slotted spoon, place tortelli in the essence and drizzle over white truffle oil.

GRASSY SAUVIGNON BLANC IS THE IDEAL SELECTION. THE ASPARAGUS FLAVOUR THAT IS SO APPARENT IN YOUNG, FRESH SAUVIGNON BLANC WILL REINFORCE THE ASPARAGUS STUFFING. A WINE THAT IS ALSO DRY AND QUITE ACIDIC AT THE FINISH IS SUGGESTED AS THIS WILL BALANCE THE STARCHY CHARACTER OF THE PASTA.

24. SEARED SARDINE FILLETS WITH A TOMATO – FENNEL STEW & GREEN OLIVE TAPENADE

25. PUMPKIN TORTELLINI WITH MUSTARD FRUITS & CITRUS BUTTER

27. PRAWN & BASIL RAVIOLI WITH A SMOKED TOMATO SAUCE

ingredients

1 quantity pasta dough (p.161)
1 egg, beaten
extra-virgin olive oil

filling
4 ripe tomatoes
1 small onion, finely diced
1 clove garlic, minced
2 tablespoons olive oil
150 ml (5 fl oz) chicken stock (p.158)
500 g (1 lb) small-medium green prawns
2 tablespoons chopped basil
1 egg
125 ml (4 fl oz) pure cream
salt and freshly ground white pepper

MATURE RIESLING WITH A SLIGHTLY SWEET FINISH. THE LIME JUICE AND HONEY CHARACTERS OF MATURE RIESLING MATCH THE SUCCULENT PRAWN FLAVOUR AND IS STRONG ENOUGH TO COPE WITH THE INTENSITY OF THE SAUCE. A TRACE OF SWEETNESS AT THE BACK PALATE WILL HELP BALANCE THE ACIDITY OF THE TOMATO.

method

Set up a smoker and prepare and smoke tomatoes (see Lobster with Smoked Tomatoes, p.24). Sweat the onion and garlic in the olive oil for 5 minutes until softened but not coloured. Chop up the smoked tomatoes and add. Cook for 3 minutes and add chicken stock. Cook at a gentle simmer for 20 minutes. Purée and strain. Season and put aside.

Take the heads and shells off the prawns. Cut in half lengthways and remove any entrails. Divide the prawns in half and place half of them into the bowl of a food processor. Add the basil and pulse the motor a few times to roughly chop. Add the egg and pulse a few more times. Add the cream and pulse a few more times. Remove from the food processor and place in a medium sized mixing bowl. Cut the reserved prawn halves into half again and add to the prawn/basil mix. Season with salt and freshly ground white pepper. Mix well.

Take the pasta dough and roll out into thin sheets with a pasta machine, as for Pumpkin Tortellini (p.46). Place a rolled pasta sheet on a lightly floured bench. Spoon prawn mixture at varying intervals along the pasta sheet. Lightly brush beaten egg around each prawn mound and carefully lay another rolled pasta sheet over the top. Press down with your fingers so that each prawn mound is completely enclosed in a pasta 'cocoon'. Using a biscuit cutter, cut into rounds that do not have too much pasta around the edges.

Cook in lightly salted simmering water for 4–5 minutes, drain, toss in a little extra-virgin olive oil and serve on the smoked tomato sauce.

28. VEGETABLE FRITTO MISTO WITH TAPENADE, AIOLI AND HUMMUS

ingredients

1 small fennel bulb
4 spring onion stems
4 asparagus spears
1 small eggplant
1 small sweet potato
1 small beetroot
4 small zucchini flowers
1 small red pepper
125 g (4 oz) chickpea flour
375 ml (12 fl oz) beer
½ quantity hummus (p.164)
½ quantity tapenade (p.165)
½ quantity aïoli (p.165)

method

To prepare vegetables: thinly slice fennel into cross-sections using the core to hold together; trim whole stems of spring onion; remove woody stems of asparagus and lightly peel skin; slice eggplant 3 mm (⅛ in) thick on an angle; peel and slice sweet potato into 3 mm (⅛ in) thick rounds; peel beetroot and cut into 3 mm (⅛ in) slices, keeping washed leaves; carefully wash zucchini flowers; peel raw red peppers and cut into large pieces.

Mix the chickpea flour and beer to form a batter. A little water may be added to thin batter slightly. If a purpose-made deep-fryer is not available, use cottonseed or vegetable oil in a large saucepan, and fill to a depth of 10 cm. Heat to 190°C (380°F). Test batter with one item of vegetable. The crispy coating should be paper thin, otherwise the batter is too thick. Lightly dust all vegetables with flour before dipping in batter and frying.

Fry all vegetables, including beetroot leaves, until batter is crisp and golden. Drain well on paper towel and serve with the hummus, tapenade and aïoli as dipping sauces.

A HERBACEOUS BLEND OF SEMILLON AND SAUVIGNON BLANC. CHOOSE A LIGHT, FRESH STYLE THAT WILL HIGHLIGHT ALL THE VEGETABLE FLAVOURS. THE WINE SHOULD BE DRY WITH CRISP ACID SO THAT IT CUTS THROUGH THE BATTER.

29. CRISPED ZUCCHINI FLOWERS STUFFED WITH GOAT'S CHEESE RICOTTA ON RATATOUILLE

ingredients

1 small onion, diced
2 cloves garlic, minced
50 ml (1½ fl oz) extra-virgin olive oil
1 red pepper, diced
1 eggplant, diced
1 zucchini, diced
250 ml (8 fl oz) tomato concasse (p.163)
500 g (1 lb) goat's ricotta
60 g tiny capers
salt and pepper
18 zucchini flowers
flour
1 quantity beer batter (p.163)
cottonseed or vegetable oil for frying

method

Sauté the onion and garlic slowly in extra-virgin olive oil, until softened but without colour. Add diced pepper and cook for a further 5 minutes. Add eggplant and zucchini and cook for 5 minutes. Add tomato and continue cooking for a further 15 minutes.

Mix ricotta with tiny capers and season. Place mixture in a piping bag and fill zucchini flowers.

Heat enough oil to make a small deep-fryer. When hot enough, dust flowers with a little flour, dip in batter and quickly fry in oil. When golden and crisp, remove and pat dry with paper towel.

Spoon ratatouille on each plate. Drizzle over a little extra-virgin olive oil. Place three fried flowers on each plate.

GRASSY SAUVIGNON BLANC WITH A DRY FINISH. SAUVIGNON BLANC IS THE LOGICAL CHOICE AS IT WILL MATCH SUPERBLY WITH THE GOAT'S CHEESE AND THE GRASSY ELEMENT WILL ALSO BE COMPATIBLE WITH THE ZUCCHINI AND CAPERS. CRISP ACID AT THE FINISH WILL HELP CUT THROUGH THE TEXTURE OF THE STUFFING.

SAFFRON IS A FLAVOURING, NOT A COLOURING. A LOT OF COOKS FEEL AS THOUGH A DISH HAS TO BE TRAFFIC-LIGHT ORANGE TO JUSTIFY USING THE WORD SAFFRON IN A DISH DESCRIPTION. LEARN HOW TO USE IT PROPERLY WITH YOUR TASTEBUDS, NOT YOUR EYES.

30. CHILLI CORN SOUP WITH STEAMED CLAMS

ingredients

4 corn cobs
olive oil
1 small onion
2 bird's-eye chillies
2 cloves garlic
1 litre (1¾ pints) chicken stock (p.158)
½ bunch coriander
salt and pepper
1 roasted red pepper (p.164)
1 x 2.5 cm (1 in) knob ginger
½ stalk lemongrass
24 clams

method

Clean corn cobs of outer leaves and fibres. Stand cobs on their ends and remove kernels with a sharp knife. In a saucepan, gently heat a little olive oil. Add minced onion, garlic and chillies and sauté for 1 minute. Add corn kernels and sauté a further 1 minute. Add chicken stock and coriander leaves, bring to the boil and simmer for 15 minutes. When corn is cooked, strain liquid from the corn and reserve. Place kernels in a food processor and purée until smooth. Add stock back to puréed corn whilst motor is running to obtain a soup consistency. Season with salt and pepper to taste.

Purée roasted pepper flesh in a food processor or blender. Thin down to a saucing consistency with a little water or stock and reserve.

In a pot big enough to hold a small bamboo steaming basket, place the lemongrass, ginger and coriander stalks and roots along with 250 ml (8 fl oz) water. Bring to the boil and simmer for 5 minutes to impart flavour. Place clams in steaming basket and put whole basket in the pot. Place lid on pot and steam. Clams will be ready when they open (about 1–2 minutes).

Heat and serve soup in wide, shallow bowls. Divide clams in shells between the bowls. Drizzle with warmed red pepper cream and garnish with sprigs of coriander.

MATURE MARSANNE WITH HONEY CHARACTER AND A DRY FINISH. MARSANNE DEVELOPS A LOVELY HONEYSUCKLE TASTE AND THIS IS PERFECT FOR BOTH THE SWEETNESS OF THE CORN AND THE HEAT OF THE CHILLI. THE DRY FINISH IS ESSENTIAL FOR PREVENTING THE COMBINATION FROM BEING CLOYING.

31. JERUSALEM ARTICHOKE SOUP WITH YABBIES & SAUTÉD APPLES

ingredients

500 g (1 lb) Jerusalem artichokes
1 litre (1¾ pints) chicken stock (p. 158)
salt and freshly ground white pepper
20 live yabbies
25 g (1 oz) unsalted butter
1 cooking apple
1 teaspoon thyme leaves

method

Peel artichokes and cover with chicken stock. Bring to a boil and simmer until tender. Remove from heat, cool slightly and purée. Season with salt and pepper.

Immerse yabbies in a sink of iced water for 30 minutes to slow down their metabolism before cooking. Boil a pot of water and boil yabbies for 4 minutes. Remove from pot and peel when cool enough to handle.

Peel apple and cut into 1-cm (½-in) dice. Melt butter in a pan and sauté the diced apple until it caramelises around the edges. Drain on a sheet of paper towel.

Divide soup into 4 wide, shallow bowls. Garnish with the yabby tails, sautéd apple and sprinkle with thyme leaves that have first been toasted in a dry pan.

FRUITY CHENIN BLANC WITH A CRISP, DRY FINISH. CHENIN BLANC IS AN OFTEN-NEGLECTED WINE, WITH SOME WINE WRITERS DERIDING IT AS A NON-CLASSIC VARIETY; BUT IT WORKS PERFECTLY WITH THIS DISH. THE FRUIT FLAVOUR OF CHENIN BLANC IS LIKE FRESH GREEN APPLES SO IT WILL BLEND BEAUTIFULLY WITH THE SAUTÉD APPLE.

32. SQUAB MINESTRONE WITH GRUYÈRE TOASTS

ingredients

2 squab pigeons
2 cloves garlic
300 g (10 oz) vegetable mirepoix*
olive oil
3 over-ripe tomatoes
1.5 litres (2¼ pints) strong chicken stock (p. 158)
1 zucchini
6 baby carrots
1 stick celery
1 small fennel bulb
100 g (3½ oz) green beans
2 ripe tomatoes
200 g (7 oz) cooked white beans
1 small baguette
100 g (3½ oz) gruyère

***Vegetable mirepoix is the name given to a roughly chopped mixture of vegetables – such as carrots, onions, celery and root vegetables – that is often used as the basis of stocks and sauces.**

LIGHT, FRAGRANT PINOT NOIR. THE GAMEY FLAVOUR OF PINOT NOIR IS A SUPERB COMPANION FOR THE RICH SQUAB FLAVOUR. THE WINE SHOULD BE LIGHT AND DELICATE SO THAT IT WILL NOT WEIGH DOWN THE SOUP.

method

Soak the white beans overnight and the next day drain, cover with fresh water and bring to the boil. Simmer until tender, about 2 hours. Drain and set aside.

Preheat oven to 220°C (435°F). In a heavy pan, seal the squab and roast them for approximately 6–7 minutes, until the breast is just rare. Allow to cool, then take the breast off the bone and reserve. Chop up the carcasses and the legs with a cleaver or heavy cook's knife. In a heavy pot, sauté the garlic and the mirepoix of vegetables in a little olive oil. Add the squab bones, chopped over-ripe tomatoes and the chicken stock. Bring ingredients to the boil and simmer for at least 1 hour to impart squab flavour through the stock. Strain and reserve stock.

Blanch zucchini, carrot, celery, fennel and green beans separately in boiling salted water and refresh under running cold water so they are all cooked to their prime. Dice all these vegetables and tomatoes; add them all plus the cooked white beans to the stock and bring back to the boil. Simmer for 1 minute, season with a little salt, and ladle into shallow broad serving bowls.

Gently reheat squab breast in a medium oven until just warmed, slice finely and place across the top of the soup. Crack some fresh pepper over the top. Serve with some crusty baguette that has been sliced on an angle, lightly toasted, topped with grated gruyère cheese and grilled.

33. CURRIED DHAL SOUP WITH SEARED SCALLOPS & CORIANDER YOGHURT

ingredients

440 g (14 oz) chickpeas
1 onion
2 cloves garlic
olive oil
1 tablespoon turmeric
1 tablespoon ground cumin
1 tablespoon brown mustard seeds
6 curry leaves
1 litre (1¾ pints) chicken stock (p. 158)
250 ml (8 fl oz) coconut milk
1 small bunch coriander
150 ml (5 fl oz) natural yoghurt
salt and pepper
24 scallops, with orange roe attached

method

Wash chickpeas under cold water and drain. Soak overnight in water.

Next day, roughly chop the onion and garlic and sweat in a little olive oil for 2 minutes. Add turmeric, cumin, mustard seeds and curry leaves and sauté for a further 2 minutes, adding a little more olive oil if necessary. Drain the chickpeas and add them to the sautéd aromatics. Mix for 30 seconds, then add the chicken stock. Bring to the boil and simmer until chickpeas are tender (1½–2 hours).

In a food processor or blender, purée the mixture to form a smooth thick soup. Add the coconut milk and season to taste. Adjust soup consistency, if a little too thick, with more chicken stock.

Finely chop the coriander. Place in a piece of muslin cloth and twist over a bowl containing the yoghurt. A couple of teaspoons-worth of coriander juice should be extracted and then mixed in with the yoghurt. Add the chopped coriander and stir in. Season lightly.

In a bowl, toss the scallops in a little olive oil. Heat a black cast-iron pan to smoking point and sear the scallops for no more than 20 seconds. Divide the soup between 4 wide, shallow bowls, drizzle over the coriander yoghurt and top with the scallops.

FRAGRANT GEWÜRZTRAMINER OR RIESLING WITH A STEELY FINISH. THE BEST GEWÜRZTRAMINERS ARE SPICY AND FLORAL ON THE NOSE BUT HAVE A VERY DEFINED SPINE-TINGLING ACID AT THE END. THIS STYLE OF WINE SUITS THE DISH AS THE FRAGRANCE OF THE CURRY CRIES OUT FOR AN AROMATIC WHITE, BUT THERE NEEDS TO BE PLENTY OF ACID AT THE FINISH TO PREVENT THE SOUP OVERPOWERING THE WINE.

29. CRISPED ZUCCHINI FLOWERS STUFFED WITH GOAT'S CHEESE RICOTTA ON RATATOUILLE

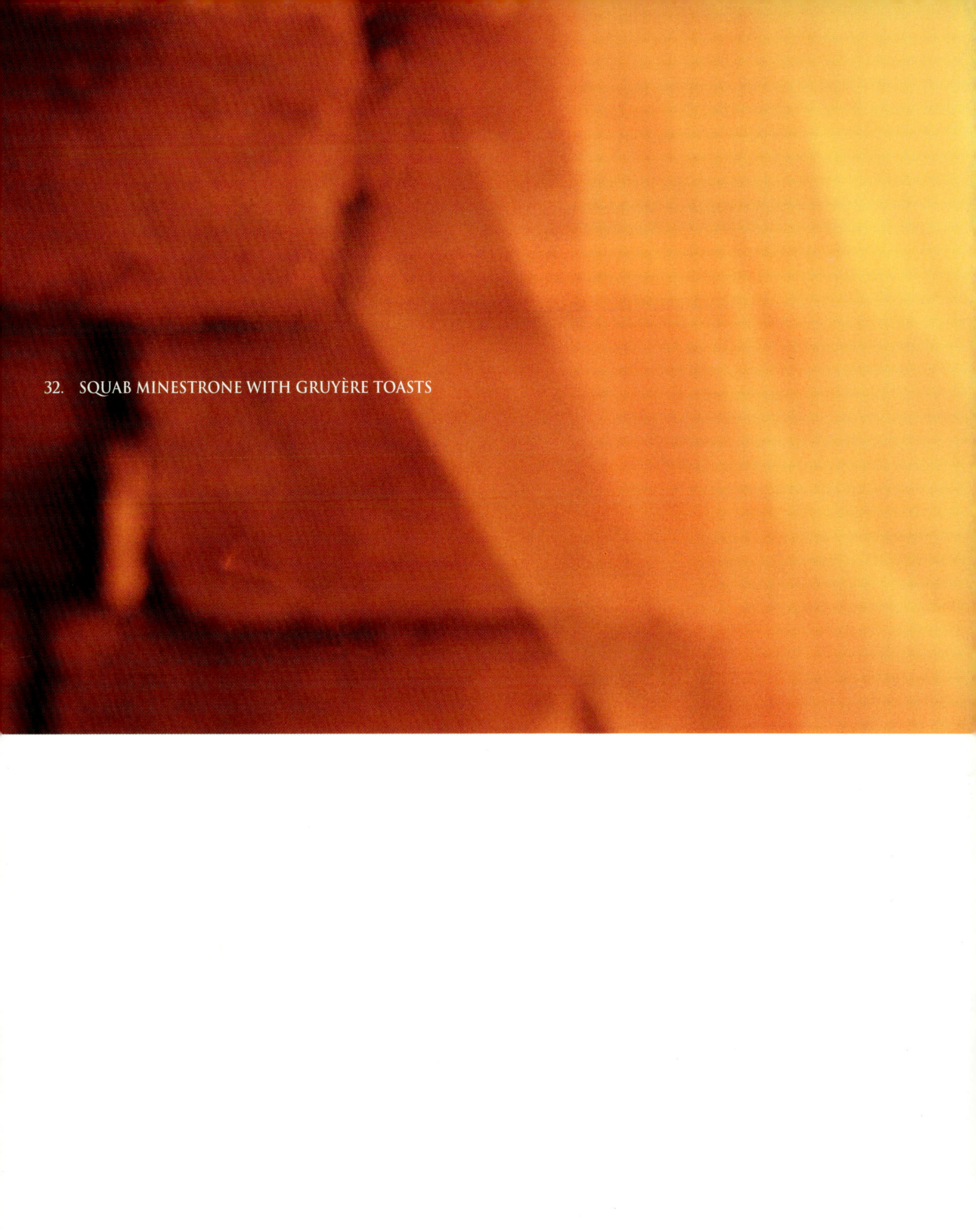

32. SQUAB MINESTRONE WITH GRUYÈRE TOASTS

34. CHAR-GRILLED BABY OCTOPUS ON CHAR-GRILLED VEGETABLES WITH A BALSAMIC DRIZZLE

ingredients

500 g (1 lb) baby octopus
100 ml (3½ fl oz) olive oil
2 cloves garlic, chopped
juice of 2 limes
freshly cracked black pepper
1 red pepper
1 green pepper
1 yellow pepper
1 small eggplant
1 zucchini
1 small Spanish onion
4 tablespoons extra-virgin olive oil
2 tablespoons balsamic vinegar
½ bunch coriander

method

Remove the head of the baby octopus and gently prise out their little beaks with the tip of a paring knife. Reserve heads for use in another dish.* Place rest of octopus in a bowl with olive oil, garlic, lime juice and plenty of cracked black pepper. Leave to steep for at least 2 hours at room temperature.

Cut peppers into quarters and trim off the ribs. Slice eggplant into 5-mm (¼-in) rounds. Cut zucchini on an angle, 5 mm (¼ in) thick. Peel onion and cut into wedges, as you would a tomato, using the base to keep the layers together.

Drain the baby octopus of most of the oil to avoid flaring, and the nasty taste that goes with it. Place the octopus on the char-grill. Brush the vegetables with the liquid drained from the octopus and also place on the char-grill. Rotate all items on the barbecue so that they are all ready at the same time, without moving them around too much (each item should only be moved once and that is when it is being turned). If you don't have a char-grill sear the food quickly in a hot, heavy frypan smeared with a little oil.

On each serving plate, arrange 1 piece of each vegetable. Place the baby octopus on the vegetables. Drizzle each plate with some extra-virgin olive oil and balsamic vinegar. Garnish with sprigs of coriander and grind over some fresh black pepper.

*Clean the octopus head of its contents. Braise the head in red wine and serve with linguine.

FRUITY SAUVIGNON BLANC WITH A SOFT ACID AND SLIGHTLY SWEET FINISH. THIS STYLE OF WINE WILL SUIT BOTH THE OCTOPUS AND THE VEGETABLES BUT IT NEEDS TO BE SWEET AND SOFT IN ACID, SO THAT IT WILL NOT CLASH WITH THE VINEGAR.

35. COULIBIAC OF ATLANTIC SALMON WITH CHIVE BEURRE BLANC & SALMON ROE

ingredients

1 fillet Atlantic salmon (about 800 g/1½ lb)
150 g (5 oz) smoked salmon offcuts
2 egg whites
salt and pepper
100 ml (3½ fl oz) cream
1 small bunch spinach
12 slices smoked salmon
1 quantity brioche dough (p.160)
1 egg, beaten
1 quantity beurre blanc (p. 166)
2 tablespoons chopped chives
40 g (1½ oz) salmon roe

method

Remove all bones from salmon fillet with tweezers or small pliers, and skin completely. Trim 8 cm (3 in) of flesh from the tail and 3 cm (1¼ in) of flesh from the rib/flap section (this trimming is done to make the thickness of the flesh even for uniform cooking). Place trimmings and the smoked salmon offcuts in the workbowl of a food processor. Run the motor for 5–10 seconds before adding 1 egg white. When mixed add other egg white. Transfer mixture to a bowl and fold in cream. Season lightly, and refrigerate.

Wash the spinach twice to remove all grit, and wilt by immersing in simmering water for 5 seconds. Refresh in ice water, remove and pat dry.

Place the trimmed salmon fillet on a workbench. Cover the upper side of the fish with wilted spinach a leaf at a time. When this side of the fish is covered, place plastic wrap over the whole fish and carefully invert. Cover the second side of the fish with spinach also. The entire fish should be covered by a thin layer of wilted spinach.

With a palette knife, spread a thin layer of smoked salmon mousse over one side of the fillet. Cover mousse with a single layer of smoked salmon. Cover the whole production with a sheet of plastic wrap and invert. Remove the plastic wrap from the top of the fillet and repeat the process of spreading the mousse and topping with smoked salmon. The entire fillet should now be surrounded by a single layer of spinach, smoked salmon mousse and smoked salmon. Completely enclose in plastic wrap and refrigerate.

Preheat oven to 220°C (430°F). On a floured workbench, roll out the brioche dough to 5 mm (¼ in) thick, and in a shape that will enclose the entire fillet in one piece. Put the wrapped fillet on the dough and fold up the sides to cover completely. Place on a non-stick tray seam side down, tuck in the ends to tidy up and brush lightly with eggwash.

Leave fish in a warm part of the kitchen for 10 minutes, then place in preheated oven. Bake for 10 minutes then reduce heat to 190°C (380°F) for a further 10 minutes.

Coulibiac is ready when the outside is golden brown and crusty, and the inside is cooked, not doughy. The fish itself should be opaque, but can be cooked more if necessary. Slice the coulibiac as you would a loaf of bread, and plate. Gently heat sauce up slightly, remove from heat and stir in chives and salmon roe. Spoon sauce around the coulibiac.

MEDIUM-BODIED AND NUTTY CHARDONNAY. THE FLAVOUR OF CHARDONNAY FRUIT IS JUST PERFECT WITH SALMON, WHICH IS GENERALLY SUITED TO THE RICHEST BARREL-FERMENTED STYLES. HOWEVER, THIS DISH REQUIRES A WINE WITH A CRISP FINISH SO THAT THE BUTTER IN THE SAUCE DOES NOT SWAMP THE WINE.

36. POTATO, ARTICHOKE & MASCARPONE PIE

ingredients

4 artichokes
1 lemon
6 medium to large potatoes
25 g butter, softened
200 g (6½ oz) mascarpone
200 ml (6½ fl oz) cream
sea salt and freshly ground black pepper
50 g (1½ oz) parmesan, grated

SWEET, FRUITY WINE WITH A SOFT FINISH. THE BEST CHOICE WOULD BE A RICH PINOT GRIGIO. ARTICHOKE IS AN ETERNAL ENEMY OF WINE, PARTICULARLY THOSE WITH OAK TREATMENT. WITH THE ADDITION OF POTATO AND MASCARPONE, THE PUNGENCY OF THE ARTICHOKE IS DISTRIBUTED THROUGH THE DISH, BUT IT IS STILL NECESSARY TO CAREFULLY SELECT A WINE WITH GREAT DEPTH AND INTENSITY.

method

Trim the artichokes of their tough outer leaves and run a vegetable peeler very lightly over the stems. Keep as much of the stalk as possible – I feel this is the best part of the artichoke. In a pot large enough to submerge the artichokes, bring some lightly salted water to the boil. Cut the lemon in half and squeeze the juice into the boiling water, then toss in the squeezed remains. Place artichokes in the water and cover with a plate to keep them completely submerged. Simmer for about 30 minutes or until tender. Test by inserting a paring knife into the heart of the artichoke. Cool and cut off the ends of the artichokes to discard the tough tips. Remove any other outer leaves that you feel may be a bit tough. Slice crossways into rounds and put aside.

Peel the potatoes and slice very fine (1–2 mm/¹⁄₁₆ in) on a mandolin if you have one.

Brush butter over the bottom and sides of a 20-cm (8 -in) black cast-iron pan. Arrange the potato slices slightly overlapping to completely cover the bottom and sides. On the potato layer, make an artichoke layer using the slices from 1 artichoke. Take a quarter of the mascarpone and dot the areas between the artichoke rings. Drizzle over some cream and season with sea salt and freshly ground black pepper. Cover with more sliced potatoes and repeat the layers until the pie is approximately 3 cm (1¼ in) thick. The last layer should be potato. Spread a little running cream over and sprinkle with grated parmesan cheese.

Preheat oven to 200°C (400°F). Cover pie with foil and bake for 30 minutes. Remove the foil for the last 5 minutes to lightly brown the top layer. Cut into wedges and serve as an entrée or as an accompaniment to a main course.

37. SAFFRON POTATO GNOCCHI WITH CLAMS & ASPARAGUS

ingredients

600 g (1¼ lb) potatoes
½ teaspoon saffron strands
100 g (3½ oz) flour
100 ml (3½ fl oz) white wine
3 sprigs thyme
2 bay leaves
300 g (9½ oz) clams
200 g (6½ oz) asparagus
200 ml (6½ fl oz) cream
picked chervil

method

Wash the potatoes, place in a large saucepan whole with skins on and cover with cold water. Bring to the boil over medium heat and simmer until tender. Drain and peel whilst hot – using rubber gloves if necessary. Place potato on a workbench and add saffron. Using an old-fashioned potato masher, work the saffron into the potato and at the same time mashing the potato into a smooth pulp (if the potato seems a bit wet at this stage, return to saucepan and dry out over low heat). Add half the flour and work into the potato.

The idea with gnocchi is to use the starch in the potato as much as possible and the starch in the flour as little as possible to make the gnocchi hold together when poaching. For this reason, add a little flour at a time and test between additions for the gnocchi's ability to hold together.

Test a gnocchi by taking a small piece of dough and dropping it into lightly salted boiling water for about 1 minute. The gnocchi should be tender (if it is tough you have probably added too much flour). When you are happy with your 'tester', roll out the dough on a lightly floured workbench to form a long sausage with a 2-cm (¾-in) diameter. Cut into 2-cm (¾-in) sections and place in lightly salted boiling water. Remove from water 10 seconds after gnocchi rise to the surface. Cool in ice water, drain, toss in a little oil to stop sticking and place in a tray until required.

In a frypan place the wine, thyme and bay leaf along with 100 ml (3½ fl oz) water. Simmer for 2 minutes before adding the clams. Cover to create a steaming chamber and steam for 1–2 minutes, until all clams have opened. Strain and reserve cooking liquid. Remove clams from their shells.

Peel asparagus and cut into 2-cm (¾-in) sections. Blanch in boiling salted water and refresh.

To finish, place reserved clam steaming liquid in a pan, add cream and bring to the boil. Reheat gnocchi very quickly in boiling water and add to the pan along with the clams and asparagus. Toss gently to warm the asparagus and clams, season if necessary, and serve when sauce reduces to a light coating consistency. Garnish with sprigs of chervil.

GRASSY SAUVIGNON BLANC WITH A CRISP DRY FINISH. SAUVIGNON BLANC'S TYPICAL GRASSY FLAVOUR REINFORCES THE FLAVOUR OF THE ASPARAGUS. A CRISP ACID FINISH IS RECOMMENDED AS IT WILL CUT THROUGH THE STARCHINESS OF THE GNOCCHI AND HIGHLIGHT THE MARITIME TANG OF THE CLAMS.

35. COULIBIAC OF ATLANTIC SALMON WITH CHIVE BEURRE BLANC & SALMON ROE

37. SAFFRON POTATO GNOCCHI WITH CLAMS & ASPARAGUS

38. GRILLED DUCK CAKES WITH A CHILLI–MANGO SALSA

ingredients

2 ducks
2 shallots, minced
1 clove garlic, minced
1 teaspoon minced lemongrass, from tender green base of stalk
½ teaspoon ground szechwan peppercorns
½ teaspoon freshly minced ginger
2 eggs
50 g (1½ oz) rocket
50 ml (1½ fl oz) extra-virgin olive oil
1 tablespoon raspberry vinegar

salsa

1 large mango, ripe but firm
1 small red pepper
1 small Spanish onion
1 clove garlic
1 bird's-eye chilli, minced
juice of 1 lime
2 teaspoons chopped mint
freshly cracked black pepper

method

Remove meat from the ducks. Discard all skin and fat from the breasts and legs. Cut the breast meat into 1-cm (½-in) dice. Take the leg meat off the bone, mince and add to the diced breast in a mixing bowl. Add the shallots, garlic, lemongrass, ground szechwan pepper, ginger and eggs. Mix very well and form into patties. Cover and refrigerate.

Stand mango on its end and with a large, sharp knife cut either side of the large pip. Try and cut as close to the pip as possible so that not too much flesh is left on it. You should have 2 'lobes' of mango with skin still attached. Insert the point of a large kitchen spoon between the skin and the flesh and carefully work the skin off. Cut the mango flesh into 1 cm (½ in) dice. Roast red pepper (see p.164), then peel and dice into 5-mm (¼-in) dice and add to the mango dice. Finely chop the onion and add. Add garlic, chilli, lime juice and chopped mint. Very gently mix all ingredients and add freshly cracked black pepper. Refrigerate for an hour to allow flavours to blend.

Heat a large, heavy frypan and moisten the bottom with a little olive oil. Cook duck cakes to medium and serve with chilli–mango salsa and rocket that has been tossed in extra-virgin olive oil and raspberry vinegar.

SWEET AND PLUMMY PINOT NOIR. PINOT NOIR WAS INVENTED FOR DUCK AND THEY SHOULD ALWAYS BE CONSUMED TOGETHER. SELECT A PARTICULARLY SWEET STYLE AS THIS WILL ALSO BLEND SUPERBLY WITH THE HEAT IN THE SALSA.

39. SAGE PAPPARDELLE WITH DUCK RAGOUT & OLIVES

ingredients

200 g (6½ oz) flour
1 bunch sage, leaves finely chopped
1 teaspoon salt
2 eggs
extra tablespoon olive oil

ragout
400 ml (13 fl oz) duck or goose fat
6 cloves garlic
4 sprigs rosemary
50 g (1½ oz) rocksalt
6 duck legs
1 onion, diced
1 tablespoon olive oil
200 ml (6½ fl oz) demi-glaze (p.159)
2 tomatoes, skinned, seeded and roughly chopped
100 g (3½ oz) kalamata olives, pitted

method

Follow the directions in the Duck and Wild Mushroom Pastie recipe (p.86) for the initial cooking of the duck in the fat.

When the duck legs are cool enough to handle, cut into 2-cm (¾-in) dice. Sweat the onion in olive oil for a few minutes without colouring and add the diced duck. Sauté for another minute and add the demi-glaze. Cook for 2 minutes and add the tomato and olives. Continue to cook slowly for a further 5 minutes and remove from heat, allowing to cool slowly to room temperature to infuse flavours.

Place the flour, sage and salt in a food processor and run the motor for about 20 seconds to evenly blend. With the motor still running, add the eggs one at a time. Add the olive oil. Stop the motor and feel the texture of the flour. It should be moist and granular. If you feel it is too dry to form a dough, add a little water and run motor to incorporate. Tip contents out on to a workbench and knead to form a dough. Continue to knead for a few minutes to build up the elasticity in the dough. Divide the dough in half and cover with a damp cloth. Clamp a pasta machine to a bench and start working one of the balls of dough through the rollers on their widest setting. Gradually decrease the setting as the dough becomes more laminated until the sheets are no more than 2 mm (¹⁄₁₀ in) thick. Cut the sheets into strips 30 cm (12 in) long and 2 cm (¾ in) wide. Hang over a broomstick or thin wooden pole to dry and repeat the process with the other dough ball. Leave sage pappardelle until required.

When ready to serve, bring a large pot of lightly salted water to the boil and cook the sage pappardelle to al dente stage. Drain. Reheat the duck ragout in a wide frypan and add the pappardelle. Toss well to coat and serve with shavings of parmesan.

A COMPLEX PINOT NOIR WITH EARTHY, FARMYARD FLAVOURS. SOME PEOPLE WOULD DERIDE SUCH A WINE AS BEING OLD-FASHIONED, BUT THE COMBINED EFFECT OF THE EARTHY CHARACTERS IN THE WINE WITH THE HEAVY, GAMEY RAGOUT IS A TASTE SENSATION, PARTICULARLY ON A COLD WINTRY NIGHT.

40. BEETROOT RISOTTO WITH KANGAROO PROSCIUTTO

ingredients

3 beetroots
1 bunch baby beetroots
50 ml (1½ fl oz) olive oil
1 onion, finely chopped
2 cloves garlic, minced
350 g (12 oz) arborio rice
200 ml (6½ fl oz) chicken stock (p.158)
75 g (2½ oz) parmesan, grated
150 g (5 oz) finely sliced kangaroo prosciutto*
16 small sage leaves

*If kangaroo prosciutto cannot be sourced, piggy prosciutto can be used.

method

Wash all beetroots under cold running water. Cut large beetroots into quarters and put through a vegetable juicer. Cook baby beetroots in acidulated water until tender. Cool, peel and quarter.

In a heavy frypan, heat the olive oil and add onion and garlic. Sauté without colouring for 30 seconds. Add rice and stir to coat grains with oil. Add 250 ml (8 fl oz) beetroot juice and simmer. Stir occasionally to prevent rice sticking. When the juice is nearly absorbed, add another 250 ml (8 fl oz), until beetroot juice has finished. If more liquid is required to finish the risotto, use the chicken stock. Toss through baby beetroots to warm through. Stir through grated parmesan. Divide the risotto between 4 bowls and top with ribbons of very thinly sliced kangaroo prosciutto. Garnish with sage leaves that have been shallow fried in olive oil to crisp.

EARTHY, RICH PINOT NOIR. THE FLAVOUR OF BEETROOT IS VERY SIMILAR TO FULLY RIPE PINOT NOIR. THE WINE NEEDS TO BE FAIRLY FULL-BODIED AS KANGAROO HAS A STRONG, SLIGHTLY GAMEY FLAVOUR.

41. ROAST QUAIL & SPRING PEA RISOTTO

ingredients

6 large quails
12 sage leaves
100 g (3½ oz) unsalted butter
salt and freshly ground black pepper
1 small onion, finely chopped
2 cloves garlic, chopped
100 ml (3½ fl oz) olive oil
350 g (12 oz) arborio rice
1 litre (1¾ pints) chicken stock (p.158)
150 g (5 oz) spring peas
50 g (1½ oz) parmesan shavings

method

Preheat oven to 220°C (430°F). Rub the cavities of each quail with a few sage leaves and smear unsalted butter over the skin. Season and brown quails in a hot pan before transferring to a roasting tray. Roast in oven for 5 minutes. When cool, remove breasts and legs from carcasses with a sharp knife. Cut breasts in half and strip meat off the leg bones. Place all bones in a pan and cover with the chicken stock. Bring to a boil, skim and simmer for 30 minutes. Strain and reserve.

Cook peas in lightly salted water for 2 minutes if they are true spring peas – older peas will require a little more cooking. Refresh in iced water.

In a non-stick frypan, sauté the onion and garlic in olive oil for 1 minute, making sure not to colour them. Add arborio rice and sauté a further 30 seconds, again without colour. Add 250 ml (8 fl oz) quail stock and simmer until almost absorbed. Add a similar amount of stock and repeat the process. Keep stirring to avoid the rice sticking to the pan. Add stock as required until the rice is cooked. It will be firm but not crunchy; soft but not mushy. Sounds confusing, but through experience you will know what I mean.

Remove pan from the heat and add quail and peas, tossing to warm gently. Season with salt and freshly ground pepper, plate up and top with shavings of parmesan cheese.

There are a few different schools of thought regarding risotto. I like my risotto to keep its shape when spooned onto a plate, as opposed to the 'porridge' look that almost appears soupy. If you like your risotto a little richer in flavour, add some butter at the end of cooking. There is no right way or wrong way with risotto, just your way.

FRAGRANT, LIGHT AND SUPPLE PINOT NOIR THE DELICATE AND GAMEY CHARACTER OF THE WINE WILL BLEND WITH THE GAMEY FLAVOUR OF THE QUAIL AND THE HIGH ACID FINISH WILL BALANCE THE CREAMY TEXTURE OF THE RISOTTO.

39. SAGE PAPPARDELLE WITH DUCK RAGOUT & OLIVES

40. BEETROOT RISOTTO WITH KANGAROO PROSCIUTTO

42. BLACKENED QUAIL WITH A GREEN PAWPAW SALAD

ingredients

4 large quails
1 litre (1¾ pints) cottonseed or vegetable oil

marinade

4 large red chillies
1 x 2.5 cm (1 in) knob ginger
1 stalk lemongrass
2 cloves garlic
1 tablespoon chopped coriander root
50 ml (1½ fl oz) soy sauce
50 g (1½ oz) red bean paste
1 tablespoon sesame oil

salad

2 cloves garlic
4 small chillies
2 tablespoons dried shrimp
100 g (3½ oz) young green beans, cut on the angle, 1 cm (½ in) long
1 ripe roma tomato, halved, seeded and diced
250 ml (8 fl oz) grated green pawpaw
2 tablespoons unsalted peanuts
1 tablespoon fish sauce
2 tablespoons lime juice
2 teaspoons palm sugar

method

To make the marinade, place chillies, ginger, lemongrass, garlic and coriander root in the workbowl of a food processor and mince to a fine paste. Add the soy, bean paste and sesame oil. When mixed, rub this paste over the quails including the body cavities. Refrigerate for 8–12 hours before cooking.

To make salad, place garlic, chillies and dried shrimp in a food processor and blend to a fine mince. Put in a bowl with the beans, tomato, pawpaw and peanuts. In a separate bowl, combine the fish sauce, lime juice and palm sugar and warm gently to dissolve the sugar. Mix the dressing with the salad 5 minutes before you intend to serve.

Heat the oil in a saucepan or wok and deep-fry the quail. Because of the marinade, the skin of the quail will blacken fairly quickly. The quail should be fried to a point where the flesh is still pink on the bone – about 8 minutes. Don't let the blackened skin fool you into undercooking the quail.

Serve the quail either whole or halved, with the green pawpaw salad.

SWEET AND LUSCIOUS PINOT NOIR. THIS IS A DISH WITH POWERFUL SPICE FLAVOURS AND REQUIRES A WINE THAT HAS SWEETNESS AND DEPTH OF FRUIT FLAVOUR IN ORDER TO BALANCE THE SHARPNESS OF THE SPICE AT THE END OF THE DISH.

43. BBQ QUAIL WITH ZUCCHINI FRITTERS & THYME HOLLANDAISE

ingredients

4 quails, boned
2 zucchini
1 egg
30 g (1 oz) parmesan, grated
100 g (3½ oz) breadcrumbs
125 ml (4 fl oz) white wine vinegar
125 ml (4 fl oz) white wine
1 small onion, diced
2 bay leaves
1 teaspoon black peppercorns
½ bunch thyme
2 egg yolks
200 ml (6½ fl oz) clarified butter
50 g (1½ oz) rocket, washed and dried
250 ml (8 fl oz) tomato concasse (p.163)

method

Place vinegar, wine, onion, bay leaves, peppercorns and thyme in a saucepan and reduce by three-quarters. Put egg yolks and reduction in a copper bowl and whisk over heat until mixture thickens to form a sabayon (if you don't have a copper bowl you will have to cook the sabayon over a double boiler to prevent it scrambling). Season and put aside in a warm place.

Grate zucchini and put in a bowl with parmesan and egg. Season lightly. Heat a non-stick frypan and add a little clarified butter. With your hands form 12 little patties out of the zucchini mixture. Sprinkle these with breadcrumbs and slowly pan-fry until golden brown. Set aside.

Lightly season quail and grill a couple of minutes each side until cooked but slightly underdone.

On each plate, place 2 zucchini fritters. Lightly dress the rocket leaves and place on top of the fritters. Cut each quail into quarters and place on the rocket. Smatter with thyme hollandaise and sprinkle with diced tomato. Finish with some freshly ground black pepper.

FRAGRANT, LIGHT AND SUPPLE PINOT NOIR. A LIGHTER STYLE OF PINOT NOIR IS PREFERRED HERE BECAUSE IT HAS THE PERFUME TO COMPLEMENT THE AROMATICS OF THE THYME AND THE VEGETABLE CHARACTER TO MATCH WITH THE ZUCCHINI, YET ALSO HAS A GAMEY QUALITY TO SUPPORT THE QUAIL.

44. POTATO PANCAKES WITH SWEETBREADS & MORELS

ingredients

500 g (1 lb) potatoes
500 ml (16 fl oz) milk
3 whole eggs
4 egg whites
75 g (2½ oz) flour
salt and freshly ground white pepper
500 g (1 lb) veal sweetbreads
100 g (3½ oz) fresh morels
100 g (3½ oz) unsalted butter
1 teaspoon chopped tarragon
200 ml (6½ fl oz) reduced veal stock (p.158)

GAMEY, MEDIUM-BODIED PINOT NOIR WITH CRISP ACID AND LOW TANNIN. THE SWEETBREADS WILL ABSORB THE NUTTY CHARACTER OF THE MUSHROOMS AND THIS FLAVOUR IS IDEAL WITH PINOT NOIR, ESPECIALLY IF IT IS GAMEY AND NOT LADEN WITH SWEET FRUIT. THE CRISP ACID AT THE FINISH WILL BALANCE THE CREAMY TEXTURE OF THE SWEETBREADS.

method

Place the potatoes whole in lightly salted water and simmer until tender. Peel while they are hot and put in the bowl of a food processor. With the motor running, add the milk. Add the eggs and egg whites one at a time until a smooth batter is formed. Add flour (as much as possible, the starch from the potato and the eggs are being used to 'set' the pancakes, so use as little flour as you can). Stop motor as soon as flour is incorporated. Cook a small pancake to test for 'setability' and add more flour if necessary. Remove mixture from bowl and season with salt and freshly ground white pepper.

Soak the sweetbreads in cold water for a few hours. Cut away any fat or connective tissue. Place in a saucepan and cover with water. Bring to the boil and simmer for 20 minutes. While hot, place sweetbreads on a plate and place another 4 plates on top as a weight. Cool completely. Slice sweetbreads 5 mm (¼ in) thick.

Heat a little olive oil in a large non-stick frypan and spoon in dollops of potato pancake batter. The dollops should spread to a diameter of about 6 cm (2½ in) and be quite thin. Don't allow the edges of the pancakes to touch each other. Brown quickly and turn over to brown the other side. 8 pancakes are required for this recipe, but I dare you not to eat any as you cook them.

Cut the morels in half lengthways and carefully wash to remove any soil. Pat dry with paper towel. Dust sweetbreads with flour. In a non-stick skillet, slowly melt 50 g of the butter. Turn up the heat and when the butter starts to foam, add the slices of sweetbread. Sear for 30 seconds each side then remove to a plate. Add the remaining butter to the pan, then the morels and tarragon. Sauté for 1 minute. Add the veal stock and reduce to a sauce consistency. Season to taste.

Place 2 potato pancakes on each plate. Lay 1 or 2 slices of sweetbread, depending on their size, over each pancake. Spoon a small amount of morels on top, allowing a little sauce to pool around the pancakes.

I AM NOT A PERSON WHO LIVES IN MODERATION. I ENJOY ALL THE BAD THINGS IN LIFE THAT NARROW-MINDED CHRISTIANS ABHOR. HEDONISTIC MAYBE, BUT TO ME IT'S PART OF A WELL-BALANCED EXISTENCE. SACRILEGE IS CONSUMING POOR QUALITY 'STUFF', BE IT FOOD, WINE – OR ANYTHING.

45. DUCK & WILD MUSHROOM PASTIE WITH WHITE BEAN MASH

ingredients

200 g (6½ oz) white beans
750 ml (24 fl oz) chicken stock (p.158)
3 cloves garlic
400 ml (13 fl oz) duck fat
2 sprigs rosemary
4 cloves garlic, smashed
60 g (2 oz) rocksalt
100 ml (3½ fl oz) olive oil
2 tablespoons diced shallot
160 g wild mushrooms in season (oyster, shiitake, cépes, morels)
½ teaspoon thyme leaves
200 ml (6½ fl oz) demi-glaze (p.159)
500 g (1 lb) puff pastry
1 egg, beaten

method

Rinse the white beans and soak in water overnight. Drain, place in a saucepan and add the chicken stock and 3 cloves garlic. Bring to the boil and simmer until tender (about 1 hour). Purée and season. Reserve.

Place duck fat in a large, heavy saucepan over low heat. Add the rosemary, smashed garlic and rocksalt. Add 125 ml (4 fl oz) water and increase the heat. Simmer for 5 minutes before adding the duck legs. Continue simmering for a further 30 minutes adding 125 ml (4 fl oz) water every 10 minutes or so when you think the previous addition may have evaporated (the water will stop the fat from frying and therefore drying the duck legs). Remove duck legs from fat and squeeze to check for tenderness. When cooled, cut meat from the bone and dice into 1.5-cm (½-in) chunks.

Gently heat olive oil in a pan. Add shallot and sauté for 2 minutes without colouring. Turn up the heat to high and add the mushrooms. Sauté for another minute, adding a little more olive oil if necessary. Add the diced duck and thyme. Sauté a further 2 minutes. Add the demi-glaze and reduce until it binds all the ingredients but is not too sticky or over-reduced. Season with ground black pepper and cool completely.

Roll out puff pastry to a thickness of 4 mm (¼ in) and cut 4 rounds each of diameter 15 cm (6 in). Spoon an appropriate amount of cold duck filling onto the centre of each pastry disc, bring up sides and form a Cornish-style pastie by pinching and crimping the pastry along the top seam. Refrigerate for 30 minutes.

Preheat oven to 200°C (400°F). Brush pasties with beaten egg and bake for 15 minutes. Serve with a dollop of hot white bean mash.

FULL-BODIED PINOT NOIR WITH FLAVOURS OF THE FOREST. THIS DISH CALLS FOR A RICH, EARTHY WINE TO COPE WITH THE GAMEY FLAVOUR OF THE DUCK AND THE INTENSITY OF THE MUSHROOMS. PINOT NOIR IS THE MOST SUITABLE VARIETY, PARTICULARLY A RUSTIC, EARTHY STYLE. THE WINE SHOULD BE FAIRLY HIGH IN ACID TO CLEAN THROUGH THE MASH.

46. ROAST DUCK BREAST ON TURNIP PURÉE WITH SPICED PEAR

ingredients

2 x 2.2–2.4 kg (about 5 lb) ducks
2 teaspoons Chinese five spice
300 ml (10 fl oz) veal stock (p.158)
3 star anise
500 g (1 lb) turnips
100 g (3½ oz) unsalted butter
2 firm pears
juice of ½ lemon
2–3 cloves
piece fresh ginger, about 5 cm (2 in) long
50 ml (1½ fl oz) white wine
100 g (3½ oz) sugar

method

Wash the ducks under running cold water, including their cavities, and pat dry with paper towel. Remove the legs and wings and save for another recipe. As much as possible, keep the skin covering the breasts. Rub the Chinese five spice into the skin and leave ducks on a bench at room temperature, preferably in a draughty place, for around 3 hours.

Preheat oven to 220°C (430°F). Set the ducks on a cake rack in a roasting tray, and roast for 30 minutes. When cool enough to handle, take the breasts off the bone. Chop up the duck bones with a meat cleaver and put in a saucepan with the veal stock and star anise. Reduce slowly to a sauce consistency and strain.

Cover the turnips with cold water in a saucepan and cook at a simmer until tender. Wearing rubber gloves, peel the turnips and roughly chop them before putting them in the workbowl of a food processor. Purée the turnips and return the purée to a clean, dry saucepan. Place over a low heat in order to incorporate the unsalted butter. If the purée is a little too moist, dry out over medium heat, making sure to stir constantly to avoid burning. Do this before adding the butter.

Peel the pears and cut in half lengthways before coring. Poach in simmering water that has been enhanced with lemon juice and cloves. Remove pears when they are cooked but still a little firm. Halve pears.

Peel the ginger and purée in a food processor. With the motor running, add the white wine and 50 ml (1½ fl oz) water. Stop the motor and scrape down the sides if necessary. Place the sugar in a heavy, small saucepan and caramelise over medium heat, swirling to avoid spot burning. On reaching caramel stage, add the ginger mixture and continue to cook for a few more minutes to form a ginger syrup. Put the pear halves cut side down on a small tray and spoon over the ginger syrup. Place under a hot grill to brown slightly.

To serve, spoon the hot turnip mash in rough oblongs onto the centre of 4 plates. Place a whole duck breast on each pile of mash and spoon over the sauce. Garnish with the spiced pear.

MEDIUM-BODIED PINOT NOIR WITH COMPLEX FLAVOURS ON THE MID PALATE BUT A HIGH ACID FINISH. I'M SURE PINOT NOIR WAS CREATED TO BE MATCHED WITH DUCK. ITS SWEET GAMEY FLAVOUR, SILKY TEXTURE AND CONTRASTING ACID FINISH MATCHES THE WEIGHT OF FLAVOUR IN DUCK AND CLEANS OUT ANY OILY, FATTY COMPONENT AT THE FINISH. THE WINE IS ALSO A GOOD MATCH WITH THE PURÉE AND THE PEAR IN THIS DISH.

47. SEARED SALT-CURED SALMON ON POTATOES MASHED WITH TRUFFLE OIL

ingredients

450 g (14 oz) sugar
500 g (1 lb) rocksalt
800 g (1½ lb) fillet of salmon
4 medium potatoes
125 ml (4 fl oz) milk
250 g (8 oz) unsalted butter
2 tablespoons white truffle oil
salt and pepper
1 roasted red pepper (p.164)
120 ml (4 fl oz) extra-virgin olive oil
2 tablespoons chopped chives

method

Mix the sugar and salt together in a bowl. Place half the mixture in a plastic tray, then place the salmon fillet on top and cover with the remaining mixture. Cover with plastic wrap, place another tray on top of the salmon and put a weight on the tray. Refrigerate for 6 hours to cure. The salmon will only be lightly cured, but this process noticeably intensifies its flavour.

After curing, remove the salmon and wash off the salt and sugar mixture. Pat dry with paper towel. Trim the cured fillet of its thin tail and rib sections (reserve the trimmings for another dish). Cut the fillet across into 4 x 150 g (5 oz) pieces, approximately 4 cm (1½ in) wide, and set aside.

Cook the potatoes, with their skins on, in boiling salted water until soft, then drain and remove the skins while they are still hot. Mash the potatoes with the milk and then whip in the unsalted butter and truffle oil.

Cut the roasted red pepper into 5-mm (¼-in) dice. Place them in a saucepan with the extra-virgin olive oil and heat gently over a low flame. Do not allow the temperature to get hot enough to fry the pepper.

If the salmon has been refrigerated, bring it back to room temperature. Heat a little oil in a frying pan and quickly sear both sides of the salmon: 20–30 seconds each side is sufficient unless you like your salmon cooked a bit more.

To serve, spoon a portion of the mashed potato in the centre of each serving plate, place a salmon piece on top, drizzle the diced pepper in oil around and sprinkle with chopped chives.

RICH, FULL-BODIED AND CREAMY CHARDONNAY WITH PLENTY OF ACID AT THE FINISH. THE SALT CURING PROCESS ADDS AN EXTRA DIMENSION TO THE TASTE OF THE SALMON. CHARDONNAY IS THE PREFERRED VARIETY DUE TO ITS GENEROSITY OF FLAVOUR. LOOK FOR THE RICHER BARREL-FERMENTED STYLES AS THEY HAVE ADDED COMPLEXITY AND RICHNESS OF FLAVOUR TO COPE WITH THE INTENSITY OF FLAVOUR IN THE DISH.

48. SARDINE PIZZA WITH GRILLED EGGPLANT & TAPENADE

ingredients

1 quantity tomato sauce (p.163)
1 eggplant
olive oil
100 g (3½ oz) pitted kalamata olives
25 g (1 oz) anchovies
25 g (1 oz) capers
2 cloves garlic
1 tablespoon chopped flat-leaf parsley
juice of ½ lemon
4 bocconcini
12 sardines
1 quantity pizza dough (p.161)

method

Place tomato sauce in a non-corrosive saucepan and reduce down further until it becomes quite thick but not quite a paste.

Slice eggplant into 5-mm (¼-in) thick slices. Sear quickly in a little olive oil in a frypan over high heat until just browned on outside.

Put olives, anchovies, capers, garlic, parsley and lemon juice in a food processor and pulse a few times to create a medium coarse mixture. Don't overmix as the tapenade will lose its sheen.

Cut off the sardines' heads. To fillet, make an incision either side of the backbone the full length of the sardine. Using your fingers, take out the backbone and as many of the tiny ribs as possible.

Preheat oven to 250°C (480°F). Roll pizza dough out into 4 rounds and transfer onto pizza trays. Spread tomato sauce over bases, but only to within 1 cm (½ in) of the edges. Top each base with eggplant, then sliced bocconcini and finally 3 sardines. Cook in oven until the base is crispy and browned, about 8–10 minutes. Top each with a dab of tapenade to serve.

FRESH UNWOODED CHARDONNAY. THE FLESH OF THE SARDINE IS WELL SUITED TO THE PEACH AND MELON OF RIPE CHARDONNAY FRUIT. IT WOULD BE WISE TO CHOOSE AN UNWOODED WINE AS THE EGGPLANT WILL OVER-EMPHASISE ANY WOOD CHARACTER. ALSO SELECT A WINE WITH PLENTY OF ACID TO BALANCE THE OILY NATURE OF THE TAPENADE.

47. SEARED SALT-CURED SALMON ON POTATOES MASHED WITH TRUFFLE OIL

49. MORETON BAY BUG PIZZA WITH CORIANDER PESTO

49. MORETON BAY BUG PIZZA WITH CORIANDER PESTO

ingredients

1 bunch coriander
2 cloves garlic
2 tablespoons pine nuts
25 g (1 oz) parmesan cheese, grated
50 ml (1½ fl oz) extra-virgin olive oil
1 roasted red pepper (p.164)
1 quantity pizza dough (p.161)
1 quantity tomato sauce (p.163)
4 bocconcini
12 cooked bug tails

method

Place the coriander, garlic, pine nuts and parmesan in a food processor. Run motor until ingredients are finely chopped and add the olive oil. Season and transfer pesto to a small bowl. Cut roasted pepper into strips.

Preheat oven to 250°C (480°F). Divide pizza dough into 4 even balls and work into pizza bases using your fingers or a rolling pin. Place each on a pizza tray and smear with tomato sauce. Cover with thinly sliced bocconcini. Cook in oven until edges and underside start to colour (about 8–10 minutes). Remove from oven and arrange halved bug tails on bases. Return to oven quickly to warm bug tails through and drizzle with coriander pesto to serve.

A GEWÜRZTRAMINER WITH AN ABUNDANCE OF SPICY, LYCHEE FRUIT AND A DRY BUT SOFT FINISH. THE SPICINESS OF THE WINE IS NECESSARY TO MATCH THE PUNGENCY OF THE PESTO'S AROMA. A FULLY RIPE GEWÜRZTRAMINER WILL HAVE THE RIGHT WEIGHT IN THE MID PALATE TO COMPLEMENT THE SUCCULENCE OF THE BUGS, WHILST A SOFTER FINISH WILL BALANCE THE TANG OF THE PESTO.

50. GRILLED CALF'S LIVER ON POMMES SARLADAISE WITH SMOKY BABA GHANNOUJ

ingredients

2 eggplants
1 teaspoon roasted garlic pulp (p.37)
50 ml (1½ fl oz) extra-virgin olive oil
200 ml (6½ fl oz) duck or goose fat
2 sprigs rosemary
½ head garlic
4 medium potatoes
1 calf's liver, no more than 1 kg (2 lb)
8 x 2 mm (⅒ in) thick slices pancetta

method

Preheat oven to 200°C (400°F). On a naked gas flame, scorch the eggplants to char the skin before placing on a tray in the oven until cooked through. This scorching gives the baba ghannouj a distinctive 'smokiness'. When cooked, cut eggplant in half and, with a kitchen spoon, scoop out flesh into a bowl. Add roasted garlic pulp and work together with the back of a fork. Stir in olive oil and season.

In a small saucepan, place the duck or goose fat with the rosemary and garlic and heat slowly over a low flame. Pour in 125 ml (4 fl oz) water and simmer until mixture stops simmering and starts to fry. At this point remove from heat and strain. (This process allows you to impart flavour into the fat. The water stops the fat from frying until the water has completely evaporated.)

Peel the potatoes and slice very fine on a mandolin. Pat dry with paper towel and place slices in a bowl with the flavoured fat; toss to coat the potatoes. Lightly coat a small 'roesti' pan or similar pan about 7–8 cm (3–4 in) in diameter with a little fat, and arrange a quarter of the potato, in overlapping slices layer upon layer, to a thickness of 1 cm (½ in). Place over medium heat until fat starts to fry. Lower heat and cook until the bottom layer of potatoes is crisped and golden. With a spatula, carefully flip over and continue to cook the other side until crisped and golden. Remove from pan, place on paper towel, and repeat the process until you have 4 'pommes sarladaise'.

With the calf's liver on a workbench, smooth side up, make a little shallow incision with a small knife to break the skin. Deftly remove the skin by running your index finger, once inserted into the incision, between the skin and the flesh, and separate them. Peel all skin off in this fashion. Slice liver on an angle 30° from the horizontal and about 4-mm (¼-in) thick. Only slice the top half of the liver as the veins and arteries in the lower half are tough and inedible; 12 good, thin slices should be able to be taken from the liver.

Place pancetta on a hot char-grill or in a hot, heavy-based pan and cook for about 20 seconds. Lightly oil calf's liver and place on a char-grill or in pan. Liver should be cooked no more than 15 seconds each side and be medium-rare; any more and the super-lean liver will be dry.

To serve, place a hot, crisp pommes sarladaise on each of 4 plates. Top with 2 slices pancetta and on that arrange 3 slices of calf's liver. Finish with a dab of baba ghannouj on top.

RICH AND SPICY SHIRAZ. SELECT A SHIRAZ FROM A WARM CLIMATE AS THESE TEND TO HAVE SPICY FRUIT BUT NOT THE OVERT PEPPER FOUND IN WINES FROM COOLER CLIMATES. THIS STYLE OF WINE SUITS THE DISH AS THERE ARE A HOST OF RICH FLAVOURS IN THE DISH ITSELF. THE SWEET FRUIT WILL ALSO PROVIDE A COUNTERFOIL TO THE SMOKINESS OF THE BABA GHANNOUJ

51. QUAIL SAUSAGE ROLL WITH VERJUS SAUCE

ingredients

4 quails
1 onion, diced
1 carrot, diced
1 stick celery, diced
olive oil
4 juniper berries
150 ml (5 fl oz) verjus or grape juice
3 teaspoons red wine vinegar
250 ml (8 fl oz) veal stock (p.158)
200 g (6½ oz) chicken fillet
1 clove garlic, minced
½ teaspoon thyme leaves
2 egg whites
50 ml (1½ fl oz) cream
salt and freshly ground black pepper
300 g (10 oz) puff pastry
1 egg, beaten

SAPPY AND FRAGRANT PINOT NOIR. QUAIL AND PINOT NOIR ARE GREAT PARTNERS BECAUSE OF THE GAMEY FLAVOURS. SELECT A LIGHTER STYLE WITH FRESH FRUITY FLAVOURS AS THIS WILL ALSO HIGHLIGHT THE PIQUANCY OF THE VERJUS SAUCE.

method

Bone the quails completely, keeping each bird completely intact as you would for a galantine. Brown the quail carcasses with the onion, carrot and celery in a little olive oil in a heavy saucepan. Add the juniper berries and then deglaze the pan with verjus (unfermented grape juice) and vinegar. Reduce by half and add veal stock. Simmer this stock for 10–15 minutes and strain through a fine mesh strainer. Reduce further until it has reached a sauce consistency. Put aside.

In a food processor, pulse the chicken a few times until a rough-textured mince has been created. Add the garlic, thyme and egg white and quickly mix until properly incorporated. Remove from food processor to a bowl and fold in the cream. Season lightly with a little salt and freshly ground black pepper.

In the middle of a large sheet of plastic wrap, place one of the boned quails, skin side down. Spoon some of the chicken mixture along the centre of the quail. Using the plastic wrap, roll the quail and its stuffing into a sausage-like shape. The quail should completely enclose the stuffing, and the plastic wrap should completely enclose the quail. Tie both ends of the plastic wrap, and repeat the process for the other 3 quails. Poach the quails in water that is barely simmering for 15 minutes. Remove from the water and cool.

Roll out the pastry to a thickness of 3 mm (⅛ in) on a bench lightly dusted with flour. Cut out shapes big enough to wrap around the quail sausage. Place a quail sausage at one end of the pastry and roll it up, sealing the join and ends with beaten egg. Repeat the process for the other quail sausages. Let the sausage rolls rest in the refrigerator for 15 minutes.

Preheat oven to 220°C (430°F). Glaze rolls with beaten egg and bake for 5 minutes, then reduce oven to 200°C (400°F) for a further 10 minutes until pastry is golden brown.

Cut each quail sausage roll in half on an angle and serve sitting in a pool of verjus sauce.

WILD MUSHROOMS ARE A SEASONAL THING. THEY SHOULD BE USED FOR THE FEW SHORT WEEKS A YEAR WHEN THEY ARE AVAILABLE FRESH, NOT FREEZE-DRIED. GLOBALLY, EVERYTHING IS OBTAINABLE ANY TIME THESE DAYS BUT OBSERVE SEASONALITY WITH ALL PRODUCE AND HAVE SOMETHING TO LOOK FORWARD TO.

51. QUAIL SAUSAGE ROLL WITH VERJUS SAUCE

54. BBQ TUNA STEAK WITH A WARM POTATO SALAD & SALSA VERDE

52. WILD MUSHROOM FRICASSÉE WITH SMOKED HARE & POLENTA

ingredients

4 hare loins, on the bone
400 ml (13 fl oz) chicken stock (p.158)
100 g (3½ oz) cornmeal
salt and pepper
100 g (3½ oz) unsalted butter
1 small onion, minced
1 clove garlic, minced
200 g (6½ oz) seasonal wild mushrooms*
1 teaspoon thyme leaves
100 ml (3½ fl oz) veal stock (p.158)
150 ml (5 fl oz) cream
flour
olive oil

LIGHT- TO MEDIUM-BODIED SHIRAZ FILLED WITH BLACK PEPPER AROMAS. COOL-CLIMATE SHIRAZ DISPLAYS SPICE AND PEPPER CHARACTERS WHICH WOULD BE THE PERFECT ACCOMPANIMENT TO THE SMOKED HARE AND THE FOREST FLAVOURS OF THE MUSHROOMS. THE WINE SHOULD ALSO HAVE CONSIDERABLE ACIDITY TO CUT THROUGH THE POLENTA.

method

In order to smoke foods, it is not necessary to buy a smoker. One can be easily created using an old baking dish and a cake rack, or even a fish kettle. Soak 200 g (6 oz) sawdust in 250 ml (4 fl oz) water. Spread over the bottom of an old baking dish, one large enough to accommodate a cake rack. Put the hare loins on the cake rack and cover with another pan the same size, inverted, or foil to create a tight seal. No smoke should be allowed to escape. Place on a medium to high heat and smoke for approximately 15 minutes. The hare should be pink on the bone. When it is so, remove from the smoking 'chamber', and cool to room temperature.

Bring chicken stock to the boil and whisk in the cornmeal. Cook over a low heat for 20 minutes, adjust seasoning and spoon or pour into a shallow tray to a depth of 1–1.5 cm (about ½ in). Use a spatula to create an even depth if necessary. Refrigerate for 1 hour and cut into 6-cm (2½-in) squares.

Melt the butter in a large sauté pan and add onion and garlic. Sauté for 1 minute. Cut the wild mushrooms down to a uniform size if necessary. Add mushrooms and thyme and sauté for 30 seconds, tossing continually. Add the veal stock and reduce by half, then add the cream and reduce to a coating, sauce-like consistency. Adjust the seasoning.

Dust 4 polenta squares with a little flour. Heat 100 ml (3½ fl oz) of olive oil in a frypan and shallow-fry the polenta for 1 minute each side until the edges are golden brown. Place 1 polenta square on each of 4 serving plates. Spoon the mushroom fricassée over and top with smoked hare fillet that has been sliced on an angle of around 60°.

*This recipe calls for wild mushrooms. Wild mushrooms are a seasonal thing. They should be used for the few short weeks a year when they are available fresh, not freeze-dried.

53. PARMESAN CRUMBED CALF'S LIVER WITH GORGONZOLA & SILVERBEET

ingredients

200 ml (6½ fl oz) cream
1 tablespoon demi-glaze (p.159)
50 g (1½ oz) gorgonzola
50 g (1½ oz) silverbeet, torn and blanched
250 g (8 oz) fresh breadcrumbs
rind of 1 lemon, grated finely
50 g (1½ oz) parmesan, grated
60 g (2 oz) flour
2 eggs, beaten
8 slices calf's liver, 5 mm (¼ in) thick
clarified butter

method

In a saucepan place cream, demi-glaze and gorgonzola. Heat to simmer and reduce to sauce consistency. Add blanched silverbeet and season. Put aside.

Add parmesan and lemon rind to breadcrumbs. Lightly flour the liver. Dip in beaten egg, then into breadcrumb mixture. In a frypan, place a little clarified butter. When hot, put crumbed liver in and pan-fry until golden brown; turn over and remove when second side is golden brown. Liver should be pink.

Place sauce and wilted silverbeet on the bottom of a plate and put pan fried liver on top.

FULL-BODIED CABERNET SAUVIGNON WITH UP-FRONT BERRY FLAVOUR AND A FIRM FINISH. THE BERRY FLAVOURS OF RIPE CABERNET SAUVIGNON WILL HAVE ENOUGH POWER TO COPE WITH THE WEIGHT AND DENSITY OF THE LIVER, WHILST THE TANNIN AT THE FINISH WILL BALANCE THE CREAMY TEXTURE OF THE SAUCE. THE SWEET BERRY FLAVOUR WILL ALSO HAVE THE EFFECT OF SOFTENING THE SALTINESS OF THE CHEESE.

54. BBQ TUNA STEAK WITH A WARM POTATO SALAD & SALSA VERDE

ingredients

1 bunch flat leaf parsley
2 tablespoons capers
6 anchovies
3 cloves garlic
1 small Spanish onion
200 ml (6½ fl oz) extra-virgin olive oil
salt and pepper
300 g (10 oz) southern gold potatoes
100 ml (3½ fl oz) mayonnaise (p.159)
2 teaspoons seed mustard
2 teaspoons chopped chives
4 tuna steaks

method

Combine the parsley, capers, anchovies, garlic, chopped onion in a food processor and run the motor in short bursts, scraping down the sides between bursts. Add olive oil and blend. Season with salt and pepper. Refrigerate salsa verde until ready to use.

Wash the potatoes to remove the dirt. Place in a saucepan and cover with cold water. Lightly salt the water, bring to the boil and simmer gently until potatoes are just cooked, about 15–20 minutes. Test for doneness by inserting a small sharp knife.

In a medium-size bowl mix together the mayonnaise, mustard and chives. Cut the cooked potatoes in half, or quarter the larger ones, and toss in the mustard mayonnaise.

Spoon warm potato salad on to the centre of each plate and top with a tuna steak that has been barbecued for about a minute each side (or pan seared in a heavy pan with a smear of oil on the base) – it should be no more than medium-rare. Place a spoonful of salsa verde on each tuna steak and serve.

SOFT AND FRAGRANT PINOT NOIR. FISH WITH RED WINE? INDEED! TUNA HAS STRONG FLAVOURS AND TEXTURE, UNLIKE MOST FISH. IT THEREFORE REQUIRES WINE WITH CONSIDERABLY MORE SUBSTANCE THAN WHITE WINE CAN OFFER. THE FRAGRANCE OF PINOT NOIR WILL SIT VERY COMFORTABLY WITH THE FRESH TANG OF THE SALSA VERDE.

55. WHOLE DEEP-FRIED BABY SNAPPER WITH THREE-FLAVOURED SAUCE & ROOT CRISPS

ingredients

1 small sweet potato
1 beetroot
1 chinese potato
1 taro root
1 lotus root
cottonseed or vegetable oil, to deep-fry
5 cloves garlic, minced
8 chillies, minced
50 ml (1½ fl oz) peanut oil
½ bunch coriander, chopped
100 g (3½ oz) cucumber, finely diced
20 g (½ oz) palm sugar
1 tablespoon fish sauce
50 g (½ oz) tamarind paste, boiled with 300 ml (9 fl oz) water
4 baby snapper, about 400–500 g (1 lb) each

method

Peel and finely slice sweet potato, beetroot, chinese potato, taro root and lotus root (use a slicing machine or mandolin for best results). Wash and pat dry. Deep-fry until crisp and put aside.

Sauté the garlic and chilli in the peanut oil without colouring. Remove from the heat and add coriander, cucumber, palm sugar, fish sauce and tamarind mixture. Bring to the boil and cool to serve.

Score the flesh of the fish. Separate flanks by putting a toothpick or picks in the body cavity, spreading the sides apart (this will help the fish to stand upright on the plate when serving). Heat oil in deep-fryer to 180ºC (350ºF) and immerse fish. When cooked, remove fish to drain completely on paper towels. Remove the toothpicks.

To serve, spoon the sauce on to the centre of each plate. Place a whole fish, upright, on top and garnish with root crisps.

AROMATIC AND FRUITY RIESLING. THIS STYLE OF WINE IS CHOSEN PRIMARILY TO MATCH THE SAUCE, WHICH IS AROMATIC AND HAS PLENTY OF CHILLI HEAT. THE SWEETNESS OF FRUIT FLAVOUR WILL MARRY WITH THE SWEET FLESH OF THE SNAPPER, WHILST THE ACID WILL CUT THROUGH ANY RESIDUAL OIL.

55. WHOLE DEEP-FRIED BABY SNAPPER WITH THREE-FLAVOURED SAUCE & ROOT CRISPS

56. STEAMED WILD BARRAMUNDI ON A BASIL RISOTTO WITH RED PEPPER ESSENCE

56. STEAMED WILD BARRAMUNDI ON A BASIL RISOTTO WITH RED PEPPER ESSENCE

ingredients

800 g (1½ lb) red peppers
100 ml (3½ fl oz) extra-virgin olive oil
1 onion, minced
2 cloves garlic, minced
50 ml (1½ fl oz) olive oil
185 g (6 oz) arborio rice
1 litre (1¾ pints) light fish stock
2 tablespoons pesto
3 star anise
1 stalk lemongrass
4 x 200 g (6½ oz) steaks wild barramundi*

method

Juice red peppers in a vegetable juicer and reduce liquid over low heat by half. Whisk in olive oil and put aside.

Sauté onion and garlic in olive oil. Do not colour. Add arborio rice and stir with a wooden spoon for 1 minute. Add stock and cook for about 20 minutes until stock is reduced and rice cooked. Stir in pesto and season. About 5 minutes before the rice is ready, place fish in steamer and steam over boiling water that has been flavoured with aromatics such as star-anise and lemongrass.

In each of 4 large, shallow bowls, spoon in basil risotto. Place fish on top of the risotto, drizzle red pepper essence around the outside.

* Wild barramundi is available from February to May only.

FULL-BODIED CHARDONNAY WITH A CREAMY TEXTURE AND SOFT ACID AT THE FINISH. WILD BARRAMUNDI HAS A STRONG FLAVOUR AND A MOIST, RICH TEXTURE. THEREFORE IT NEEDS A BIG WINE AND BARREL-FERMENTED CHARDONNAY IS THE BEST OPTION. THE RED PEPPER ESSENCE ADDS A SPIKE, SO SELECT A WINE WITH A SOFT ACID FINISH TO BALANCE.

57. PISTACHIO CRUSTED BLUE-EYE COD WITH SAFFRON MASHED POTATOES & MASALA SAUCE

ingredients

500 g (1 lb) potatoes
125 ml (4 fl oz) milk
18 strands saffron
200 g (6½ oz) unsalted butter
150 g (5 oz) unsalted pistachio nuts
salt and freshly ground black pepper
4 x 180 g (6 oz) steaks blue-eye cod
24 leaves coriander
½ quantity masala sauce (p.166)

method

Cook potatoes, skins on, in simmering water until tender. While the potatoes are cooking, place the milk and saffron in a small saucepan and slowly bring to a boil. Remove from heat as soon as it reaches this point. Drain potatoes and, with rubber gloves on, peel off the skins. Mash potato either manually or with a food processor and add saffron milk. When fully incorporated, add unsalted butter.

Preheat oven to 190°C (375°F). Peel pistachio nuts and chop in a food processor to a rough meal. Add a pinch of salt and pepper. Cover the top of each piece of fish with a thin coating of pistachio meal and place on a lightly oiled oven tray. Bake in oven for 7 minutes.

To serve, spoon mashed potatoes on to 4 plates and top with a piece of pistachio crusted blue-eye. Pour around masala sauce and garnish with small sprigs of coriander.

MEDIUM-BODIED CHARDONNAY WITH A CRISP ACID FINISH. SELECT A CHARDONNAY THAT HAS BEEN BARREL-FERMENTED, BUT NOT OVERLY RIPE AND RICH. YOU WILL FIND THAT THIS IS A GREAT MATCH FOR THE DELICATE BUT DISTINCTIVE BLUE-EYE FLAVOUR. THE CRISP ACID AT THE FINISH IS SUGGESTED TO BALANCE THE STARCH OF THE POTATOES AND THE SWEETNESS OF THE SAUCE.

58. PAILLARD OF CHICKEN BREAST WITH PRESERVED LEMON COUSCOUS & PISTACHIO BUTTER

ingredients

50 g (1½ oz) pistachio nuts
1 bird's-eye chilli
160 g (5 oz) unsalted butter
3 tablespoons chopped parsley
3 tablespoons pomegranate seeds
2 shallots, minced
2 cloves garlic, minced
olive oil
375 ml (12 fl oz) boiling chicken stock (p.158)
300 g (10 oz) couscous
3 tablespoons finely diced preserved lemon (p.162)
salt and pepper
4 double chicken breasts (from a 1-kg bird)

method

Either dry roast pistachio nuts and chilli in a pan, or put briefly in oven, until lightly browned. Place in a food processor and pulse a few times until finely chopped but not mealy. Put in a bowl with unsalted butter and parsley. Mix together thoroughly to form a compound butter.

Purée pomegranate in a blender and strain through a fine sieve. Reduce pomegranate juice in a non-corrosive saucepan over low heat to a syrup – it will be quite tart, but this helps balance the richness of the pistachio butter.

Sweat the shallots and garlic in a little olive oil for 5 minutes. Add the chicken stock and remove from the heat. Pour this mixture over the couscous and stir. Put aside for 10 minutes. When the couscous has absorbed all the liquid and fluffed up, add the diced preserved lemons; make sure that only the skin of the lemons is used and the flesh is discarded. Adjust seasoning.

Using the side of a meat cleaver or the flat side of a meat tenderiser, lightly tap the chicken breasts to obtain a uniform thickness.

Char-grill or pan sear chicken breasts, leaving them slightly pink at the centres. Reheat couscous (a microwave is best for this). Divide the couscous between 4 plates. Place chicken on the couscous and top with a dollop of the pistachio butter. Drizzle pomegranate syrup around. The dish can be garnished with fried julienne of leek.

NUTTY, RICH FULL-BODIED CHARDONNAY. THE NUTTY FLAVOUR OF BARREL-FERMENTED CHARDONNAY IS A PERFECT COMPANION FOR CHICKEN. THE LEMON-FLAVOURED COUSCOUS PROVIDES CONTRASTING FLAVOUR AND TEXTURE. BE CAREFUL NOT TO CHOOSE A WINE WITH VERY OBVIOUS OAK MATURATION AS THE FLAVOUR OF OAK AND SPICY CHARACTERS DO NOT MIX.

59. 'BAKED IN A BAG' CHICKEN BREAST WITH PROSCIUTTO & BRAISED WITLOF

ingredients

4 skinless chicken breasts, about 180 g (6 oz) each
8 fine slices prosciutto
6 sprigs thyme
100 g (3½ oz) unsalted butter
150 ml (5 fl oz) strong chicken stock (p.158)
6 witlof
3 cloves garlic
100 ml (3½ fl oz) cream
100 ml (3½ fl oz) demi-glaze (p.159)

method

Wrap each chicken breast with 2 slices of prosciutto. Place 2 chicken breasts in each of 2 medium-sized oven bags. In each bag, put 3 sprigs thyme, 25 g (1 oz) butter and 2 tablespoons stock. Tie bags up.

Preheat oven to 190°C (375°F). Cut witlof in half lengthways and wash very gently. Melt the remaining butter in a pan. Smash the garlic cloves with the side of a large cook's knife and add to the pan. Add the witlof and gently sauté for 1 minute without colouring. Add the remaining chicken stock and season. Cover with foil and place in oven for 25 minutes. Remove from the oven and add the cream. Return to the stove top and simmer until the cream and braising juices have reduced to a light coating consistency.

Increase oven to 200°C (400°F). Place bags containing the chicken in oven for approximately 15–18 minutes. As the stock in the bag heats up, it creates steam. The bag expands and the chicken breasts cook under pressure, and therefore quicker than usual.

When cooked, strain the cooking juices into a saucepan. Add the demi-glaze and heat until reduced to a sauce consistency.

Lay 3 halves of the braised witlof, side by side, on each of 4 serving plates. Place a wrapped chicken breast crossways on the witlof and spoon a little of the brown reduction over each breast.

RICH, NUTTY, BARREL-FERMENTED CHARDONNAY WITH ONLY A SMALL AMOUNT OF MALOLACTIC FERMENTATION AND A FAIRLY CRISP ACID FINISH. THE TOASTY AND NUTTY AROMAS OF BARREL-FERMENTED CHARDONNAY BLEND PERFECTLY WITH THE VARIETY'S NATURAL STONE FRUIT AND MELON FLAVOURS. THIS COMPLEX BREW IS SUPERB WITH THE PROSCIUTTO-WRAPPED CHICKEN.

58. PAILLARD OF CHICKEN BREAST WITH PRESERVED LEMON COUSCOUS & PISTACHIO BUTTER

63. BBQ FILLET OF BEEF WITH GORGONZOLA POLENTA & RED ONION JAM

60. HAZELNUT-CRUMBED VEAL CUTLETS WITH EGGPLANT RELISH

ingredients

50 ml (1½ fl oz) olive oil
1 small onion, diced
2 cloves garlic, minced
1 x 2.5 cm (1 in) knob ginger, minced
2 chillies, minced
1 teaspoon turmeric
½ teaspoon mustard seeds
2 eggplants
125 ml (4 fl oz) red wine vinegar
90 g (3 oz) brown sugar
100 g (3½ oz) hazelnuts
1 loaf day-old bread
grated rind of 1 lemon
salt and freshly cracked black pepper
2 eggs
50 ml (1½ fl oz) milk
4 double-cut veal cutlets
125g (4 oz) flour
olive oil

MEDIUM-BODIED AND PEPPERY SHIRAZ. THE PEPPER AROMA WILL BLEND SUPERBLY WITH THE SPICY RELISH. THE WINE SHOULD NOT BE TOO RICH OR POWERFUL AS THIS WOULD OVERWHELM THE DELICACY OF THE VEAL FLESH. THERE SHOULD BE FIRM TANNINS AT THE FINISH TO CONTRAST WITH THE CRUNCHY HAZELNUT CRUMB COAT.

method

Heat olive oil in a large saucepan and add the onion, garlic, ginger, chilli, turmeric and mustard seeds. Sauté for 2 minutes without colouring. Cut eggplant into 1-cm (½-in) dice and add to the spices. Continue to sauté for a further 5 minutes. Add vinegar and brown sugar. Simmer for 20 minutes and cool. This relish will keep for 30 days, covered, in a refrigerator.

Toast hazelnuts in a dry, heavy-based pan and rub to remove as much skin as possible. Place in a food processor and finely chop, but not to a meal. Chop up loaf of bread, crust and all, and process into coarse breadcrumbs. Place in a bowl and add the chopped hazelnuts and lemon rind. Season with a little salt and freshly cracked pepper. Crack the eggs into another bowl and add the milk. Whisk together to make eggwash.

Cut one of the ribs off each of the veal cutlets. Between two sheets of plastic, lightly flatten each double cutlet using the side of a meat cleaver, to a thickness of slightly less than 1 cm (½ in). Lightly dust with flour, dip into the eggwash then crumb each cutlet.

Because of the size of the cutlets, you will have to use 2 pans to cook them, or 1 pan and only cook 2 cutlets at a time. Whatever you decide, heat some olive oil in a large frypan. When hot, and not before, add the crumbed cutlets and cook until the crumbs are golden brown before turning and cooking the other side. Once the crumbs start to colour, turn heat down to avoid burning before meat is cooked. Cutlets are ready to serve when they are golden on the outside and pink on the inside. Serve with the eggplant relish.

61. ROAST LAMB LOIN WITH WHITE BEANS & MINT PESTO

ingredients

250 g (8 oz) haricot beans, soaked overnight
1 onion, finely diced
2 cloves garlic, minced
1 tablespoon olive oil
1 zucchini, in 5 mm (¼ in) dice
1 small eggplant, in 5 mm (¼ in) dice
200 ml (6½ fl oz) demi-glaze (p.159)
3 sprigs thyme
125 ml (4 fl oz) tomato concasse (p.163)
4 mid loins of lamb, boned

pesto

⅓ bunch basil
⅓ bunch flat leaf parsley
⅓ bunch mint
100 g (3½ oz) pine nuts
3 cloves garlic
100 g (3½ oz) parmesan, grated
150 ml (5 fl oz) extra-virgin olive oil
salt and freshly ground black pepper

method

Drain beans from soaking water and cover with fresh water in a pan. Bring to the boil and simmer until beans are tender (about 1½ hours). They should be able to be squashed between the tongue and the roof of the mouth. When tender, refresh under running water.

Sauté onion and garlic in olive oil without colouring. Add diced zucchini and eggplant and sauté for a further 2 minutes. Add demi-glaze and thyme and bring to the boil. Simmer and add cooked white beans. When beans are warmed through add tomato concasse.

To make pesto, in a food processor, place basil, parsley, mint, pine nuts, garlic and parmesan. Run motor for 10 seconds and stop. Scrape down the sides and, with motor running again, slowly pour in the olive oil. Remove from workbowl of machine and season. Adjust pesto thickness with a little extra-virgin olive oil if needs be so that pesto can be smattered over the lamb.

Preheat oven to 200°C (400°F). Seal lamb loins in a frypan, then roast until they are rare, about 8–10 minutes. Rest for 5 minutes to allow meat to relax. Spoon bean mixture onto the centre of each plate with some of the sauce it was cooked in. Slice the loins across the grain of the meat and lay on the top of the beans. Smatter the pesto over the lamb.

FULL-BODIED CABERNET SAUVIGNON WITH A FIRM FINISH. THE BLACKCURRANT OVERTONES OF CABERNET GIVE A LIFT TO THE FRAGRANCE OF LAMB. THE TANNIN AT THE FINISH WILL CLEAN THROUGH THE STARCHY NATURE OF THE BEANS.

62. PEPPERED OX FILLET WITH HORSERADISH MASHED POTATOES

ingredients

500 g (1 lb) large potatoes
4 teaspoons grated horseradish
200 ml (6½ fl oz) milk
200 g (6½ oz) butter
salt and freshly ground white pepper
4 x 200 g (6½ oz) prime fillet steaks
freshly cracked black pepper
50 ml (1½ fl oz) brandy
100 ml (3½ fl oz) demi-glaze (p.159)
200 ml (6½ fl oz) cream
2 tablespoons green peppercorns

method

Leaving their skins on, bring potatoes to the boil and simmer until tender. Once cooked, peel and pass through a food mill, mix in horseradish and milk. Whip in the unsalted butter and season to taste with salt and freshly ground white pepper.

Preheat oven to 240°C (460°F). Roll the eye fillet in cracked peppercorns. Heat a heavy pan, add a little oil and seal all sides of steaks. Place in hot oven to cook to the desired stage. Remove from oven and rest in a warm part of the kitchen on a tray. Pour off any excess fat, deglaze pan with brandy and add demi-glaze, cream and whole green peppercorns. Reduce to a saucing consistency. Whilst this is happening, reheat the horseradish mashed potatoes. Place cooked fillet to one side of the plate and a spoonful of horseradish potato to the other side. Spoon the pepper sauce over the steak and serve.

WARMING, SPICY SHIRAZ WITH AN OVERLAY OF BLACK PEPPER CHARACTER. THE PEPPER IN THE WINE WILL OBVIOUSLY BE A GOOD MATCH WITH THE PEPPER CRUST ON THE MEAT, WHILST THE SPICY FLAVOURS AND MEATY TEXTURE OF THIS STYLE OF WINE IS JUST PERFECT WITH THE STEAK ITSELF.

FOOD CRITICS – YA CAN'T LIVE WITH 'EM, AND YA CAN'T SHOOT 'EM. GOOD ONES ARE FRIENDS OF THE INDUSTRY WHO WRITE EVERY WORD RESPONSIBLY. BAD ONES WOULD SEEM TO SMILE AS THEY WALK OVER THEIR GRANDMOTHER'S GRAVE.

63. BBQ FILLET OF BEEF WITH GORGONZOLA POLENTA & RED ONION JAM

ingredients

2 Spanish onions
100 g (3½ oz) unsalted butter
50 ml (1½ fl oz) red wine vinegar
100 ml (3½ fl oz) red wine
1 tablespoon cassis
200 ml (6½ fl oz) veal stock (p.158)
500 ml (16 fl oz) chicken stock (p.158)
185 g (6 oz) cornmeal
salt and pepper
200 g (6½ oz) gorgonzola or dolce latte
2 shallots, minced
1 garlic clove, minced
extra 20 g (¾ oz) unsalted butter
200 ml (6½ fl oz) red wine
200 ml (6½ fl oz) demi-glaze (p.159)
50 g (1½ oz) bone marrow
4 x 200 g (6½ oz) eye fillet steaks

method

Peel and finely slice onions. Melt butter in a heavy saucepan and sweat sliced onion slowly for 5 minutes. Add red wine vinegar and reduce by half. Add red wine and cassis and reduce by half again. Add veal stock and continue slowly cooking and reducing liquid. Total cooking time should be 25–30 minutes and onions should be soft, sticky, sweet and sour: a 'jam'.

Bring chicken stock to the boil and whisk in cornmeal. Turn heat down to a minimum and cook for 20 minutes. Remove from heat and stir in the gorgonzola. Season to taste.

In a small saucepan, sweat the minced shallots and garlic in the extra butter until soft but not coloured. Add 200 ml (6½ fl oz) red wine and reduce by half. Add demi-glaze, bring to the boil and simmer. With the back of a fork, mash the bone marrow and whisk into the simmering sauce until dissolved. Strain, and you have a sauce bordelaise.

To serve, barbecue or pan-sear steaks to required doneness. Spoon a little soft polenta on to the centre of each plate. Surround with a shallow 'moat' of bordelaise sauce. Top the polenta with a steak and top each steak with a small spoon of red onion jam.

RICH, FULL-BODIED SHIRAZ WITH PLENTY OF TANNIN AT THE FINISH. SHIRAZ IS THE IDEAL PARTNER FOR HEAVY, RICH BEEF. THE TANNIN AT THE FINISH WILL CUT THROUGH THE STARCHY CHARACTER OF THE POLENTA AND THE CREAMINESS OF THE CHEESE.

64. PAILLARD OF KANGAROO WITH SWEET POTATO MASH & RED PEPPER CHUTNEY

ingredients

1 onion, diced
2 cloves garlic, minced
1 tablespoon olive oil
2 roasted red peppers (p.164)
½ teaspoon minced fresh ginger
¼ teaspoon minced chilli
100 ml (3½ fl oz) red wine vinegar
50 g (1½ oz) brown sugar
25 g (¾ oz) raisins
100 ml (3½ fl oz) tomato sauce (p.163)
250 g (8 oz) rocksalt
300 g (10 oz) sweet potato
150 g (5 oz) unsalted butter
salt and freshly ground white pepper
4 kangaroo sirloins

method

In a saucepan, sweat the onion and garlic in olive oil for five minutes without colouring. Cut the peppers into 7 mm (⅓ in) wide strips. Add the pepper strips, ginger and chilli to the saucepan and continue sweating on a low heat for a further 5 minutes. Add red wine vinegar and brown sugar and cook for another 5 minutes, stirring occasionally to avoid sticking. Add raisins and tomato sauce and cook for 20 minutes to finish. Make this chutney at least 3 days prior to use. It will keep for 30 days, refrigerated.

Preheat oven to 180°C (350°F). On a baking tray, spread out rocksalt and place sweet potatoes on top. Bake in oven until tender. Remove from oven and cut in half lengthways to scoop out cooked flesh. Discard skins. Mash the sweet potato flesh with unsalted butter and season with salt and freshly ground white pepper.

Clean the kangaroo sirloins of any connective tissue. Make a cut lengthways on each sirloin through the centre, but not right through. This allows the meat to be butterflied. Using the side of a meat cleaver or the flat side of a meat tenderiser, lightly tap the butterflied sirloins to obtain a uniform 1-cm (½-in) thickness.

The kangaroo can either be barbecued or pan-seared. Either way, brush with olive oil and ensure the meat is at room temperature. Sear on a very hot barbecue, or in a very hot pan. Because of the roo's very low fat content, the meat should be cooked no more than medium-rare. Serve with sweet potato mash and red pepper chutney.

FULL-BODIED SWEET GRENACHE WITH A FIRM FINISH. THE ACCENTUATED SWEET RASPBERRY CHARACTER OF OLD VINE GRENACHE IS PERFECT FOR THIS DISH AS IT WILL MARRY WITH THE GAMEY FLAVOUR OF KANGAROO AND SWEETNESS OF THE CHUTNEY. A FIRM FINISH IS NEEDED TO COUNTER AND BALANCE THE STARCH OF THE MASH.

65. VENISON BURGER WITH GRILLED PINEAPPLE & CHILLI MAYO

ingredients

1 small onion, minced
2 cloves garlic, minced
600 g (1¼ lb) venison mince
200 g (6½ oz) pork fat, minced
1 tablespoon chopped sage
2 eggs
4 rings fresh pineapple
salt and pepper
8 thin slices gruyère
2 hamburger buns
50 g (1½ oz) rocket
2 vine-ripened tomatoes
1 Spanish onion, sliced into rings
1 quantity beer batter (p.163)
oil for frying
100 ml (3½ fl oz) mayonnaise (p.159)
1 teaspoon minced chillies

VANILLA-MALTED MILKSHAKE OR A SWEET, FRUITY BEER. THE RICH, GAMEY MEAT FLAVOUR COMBINED WITH THE SWEETNESS AND ACID OF THE PINEAPPLE AND THE HEAT OF THE MAYO MAKES AN EXCITING COMBINATION OF FLAVOURS. UNFORTUNATELY IT IS IMPOSSIBLE TO PICK A WINE THAT CAN NAVIGATE THROUGH THIS.

method

Sweat the onions and garlic in a little olive oil for 2 minutes on a medium heat. Cool and place in a mixing bowl with the venison and pork fat minces, sage and eggs. Mix well and season. Form into 4 large patties about 2–3 cm (1 in) thick.

In a heavy frypan, cook the venison patties in a little olive oil to a medium-rare stage. Grill the pineapple and in the last 30 seconds or so place 2 slices of gruyère on each ring to melt. Cut the hamburger buns in half and toast the 4 halves both sides. Dip onion rings in batter and deep fry.

To construct the burger, on each half bun place a small amount of rocket, followed by slices of tomato, a venison pattie, a cheesy pineapple ring and onion rings. Mix the mayonnaise and chilli together and drizzle over the whole thing.

66. RED THAI PEANUT KANGAROO CURRY WITH COCONUT RICE

ingredients

125 ml (4 fl oz) peanut oil
2 pieces cinnamon stick
1 tablespoon coriander seed
2 teaspoons cumin seed
2 teaspoons black peppercorns
10 shallots, chopped fine
6 cloves garlic, chopped fine
8 bird's-eye chillies, chopped fine
1 knob galangal, chopped fine
2 stalks lemongrass, chopped fine
½ bunch coriander root, chopped
2 teaspoons cayenne
2 teaspoons turmeric
2 teaspoons dry roasted shrimp paste
75 g (2 oz) raw peanuts, dry roasted and chopped very fine
4 red peppers
750 ml (1¼ pints) thick coconut milk
10 kaffir lime leaves
2 teaspoons salt
300 g (10 oz) long-grain rice
625 ml (1 pint) coconut milk
600-800 g (about 1½ lb) kangaroo fillet
extra 100 ml (3½ fl oz) peanut oil
150 g (5 oz) okra
150 g (5 oz) Thai eggplant

method

Heat 125 ml (4 fl oz) peanut oil and fry the cinnamon, coriander seed, cumin and peppercorns. Add the shallots, garlic, chillies, galangal and lemongrass and fry until fragrant. Add coriander root, cayenne, turmeric, shrimp paste and peanuts. Fry for a further 2 minutes. Purée the red peppers and add, along with the thick coconut milk, lime leaves and salt. Simmer for 30 minutes and strain. This recipe should yield approximately 500 ml (16 fl oz) red curry sauce.

Wash the rice under cold water and drain. Place in a heavy-based saucepan and cover with coconut milk. Cover with a lid and simmer for 20 minutes after it reaches the boil.

Heat a wok over a high heat. When very hot add a little peanut oil and sear the kangaroo for about 30 seconds, until completely sealed. Remove the kangaroo from the wok and return wok to heat. When it regains its heat add a little more peanut oil and wok-sauté the okra and Thai eggplant for about 45 seconds. Add 400 ml (13 fl oz) of the curry sauce and lower the heat slightly to simmer the sauce. Cook the okra and eggplant in the sauce for about 3 minutes. When they are cooked through, add the seared kangaroo and simmer for 1 minute together.

Serve immediately, or the kangaroo will be unpleasant to eat due to overcooking. It should be served underdone, because it is such a lean meat.

MALTY BEER WITH A CLEAN, FRESH, HOPPY FINISH. THE COMBINATION OF HOT CURRY AND THE GAMEY INTENSITY OF THE KANGAROO WOULD OVERWHELM WINE. AN ICY COLD BEER WITH SOME DRYING, SLIGHTLY BITTER HOPS CHARACTER AT THE FINISH IS VERY REFRESHING WITH THIS DISH.

67. SAGE ROASTED CHICKEN BREAST WITH GOATS CHEESE GNOCCHI

65. VENISON BURGER WITH GRILLED PINEAPPLE & CHILLI MAYO

67. SAGE-ROASTED CHICKEN BREAST WITH GOAT'S CHEESE GNOCCHI

ingredients

2 large potatoes
150 g (5 oz) strong goat's cheese
200 g (6½ oz) flour
2 x 1.6–1.8 kg (about 3½ lb) chickens
12 sage leaves
50 g (1½ oz) unsalted butter
200 ml (6½ fl oz) veal stock (p.158)
100 ml (3½ fl oz) chicken stock (p.158)
150 ml (5 fl oz) cream
1 bunch spinach, washed and coarser stems discarded

method

Follow the instructions for Saffron Gnocchi (p.67) to make the goat's cheese gnocchi. Use exactly the same method except add goat's cheese instead of the saffron. A little more flour will be needed because of the extra moisture in the goat's cheese. Cook gnocchi and set aside.

Remove the legs and wings from the chickens and reserve for another dish. Be careful to keep as much skin as possible covering the chicken so as to protect the breasts during roasting. Gently lift the skin covering each breast and place 3 sage leaves under each. Rub the butter on top of the skin covering the breasts and season with salt and pepper.

Preheat oven to 200°C (400°F). Place chicken in oven in a large, heavy pan and roast for 10 minutes before reducing heat to 180°C (350°F) for a further 15 minutes. Remove chickens from the pan and deglaze pan with veal stock. Reduce over medium heat to create flavourful juices that are not too cloying.

Reduce chicken stock by half in a pan. Reheat gnocchi by immersing in simmering water for about 1 minute and add gnocchi and cream to chicken stock. Boil and reduce the cream until it starts to coat the gnocchi. If you require a stronger goat's cheese flavour, some extra cheese can be crumbled into the cream sauce at this stage. Adjust seasoning if necessary.

Wok-sauté the spinach in a little oil and then a touch of water or stock. Place a small pile on each serving plate. Take the chicken breasts off the bone and serve 1 per person on the wilted spinach mound with the goat's cheese gnocchi. Finish by straining the reduced pan juices through a fine sieve around the chicken. Don't sauce the breasts themselves as the skins will lose the crispiness produced by the roasting.

RICH, FULL-BODIED CHARDONNAY WITH A CRISP ACID FINISH. FULL-FLAVOURED BARREL-FERMENTED CHARDONNAY IS SUGGESTED HERE AS IT MATCHES SUPERBLY THE RICH CHARACTER OF THE CHICKEN INFUSED WITH THE HERBAL TANG OF THE SAGE. THE ACID STILL NEEDS TO BE OBVIOUS AT THE FINISH TO CUT THROUGH THE GNOCCHI.

68. ROAST DUCK WITH SWEET POTATO MASH, BOK CHOY & BITTERSWEET ORANGE SAUCE

ingredients

2 ducks, about 2 kg (4½ lb) each
1 tablespoon maltose
50 g (1½ oz) sugar
2 oranges
50 ml (1½ fl oz) Grand Marnier
250 ml (8 fl oz) demi-glaze (p.159)
500 g (1 lb) rocksalt
500 g (1 lb) sweet potato
200 g (6½ oz) unsalted butter
salt and pepper
2 baby bok choy
50 ml (1½ fl oz) chicken stock (p.158)

method

Bring a large pot of water to a boil and turn down to a simmer. Holding a duck over the pot, ladle water over the duck until the skin tightens – probably about 90 seconds each. Repeat for other duck. Mix the maltose with 125 ml (4 fl oz) water and brush the skin of each duck. Hang the ducks in a well-ventilated space for 12 hours or in front of a fan for 4 hours.

Preheat oven to 220ºC (430ºF). Place ducks on a rack in a roasting tray and roast for 45 minutes, turning over halfway. Cool and take leg and breast off the carcasses. Reserve.

Caramelise sugar with a little water and add the juice from the 2 oranges to stop the caramelising process. Add the Grand Marnier and the orange skins. Bring to a simmer and add the demi-glaze. Slowly simmer and reduce. When mixture has reduced to a saucing consistency, strain and reserve.

Preheat oven to 180ºC (350ºF). On a baking tray covered with rocksalt, bake sweet potatoes until softened. Remove from oven and peel off skins. Put through a food mill or potato ricer. Place pulp in a pan and gradually incorporate butter. Adjust seasoning.

To serve, cut bok choy in half and stir-fry in a little oil and chicken stock. Place a mound of sweet potato mash just off-centre of each plate. Top with half a bok choy each and surround with bittersweet orange sauce. Reheat duck under a hot grill if necessary (make sure that the skin is crispy) and lean a breast and leg of duck on each mound.

FULL-BODIED PINOT NOIR WITH SOFT TANNIN AND HIGH ACID AT THE FINISH. LOOK FOR A PINOT THAT HAS LOADS OF SWEET FRUIT, BUT ALSO HAS BEEN GIVEN PLENTY OF OAK MATURATION TO ADD COMPLEXITY. THE FINISH IS IMPORTANT AS A TANNIC WINE WOULD ACCENTUATE THE BITTER CHARACTERS IN THE SAUCE. A LOW TANNIN/HIGH ACID FINISH WILL ADD TO THE INTENSITY AND AFTERTASTE OF THE SAUCE.

69. BAKED HAM HOCK WITH SPICY BAKED BEANS & PICKLED OKRA

ingredients

hocks

2 carrots
1 onion
4 sticks celery
4 bay leaves
4 cloves garlic
150 g (5 oz) molasses
500 ml apple cider
2 tablespoons peppercorns
4 portion-size pickled pork hocks, washed under running water for 1 hour
1 tablespoon Dijon mustard, thinned down with a little water
100 g (3½ oz) brown sugar

baked beans

200 g (6½ oz) haricot beans, soaked overnight in water
1 onion
1 clove garlic
olive oil
½ teaspoon grated fresh ginger
½ teaspoon chopped thyme
1 bay leaf
50 g (1½ oz) kaiserfleisch, diced
200 ml (6½ fl oz) sparkling ale
250 ml (8 fl oz) chicken stock (p.158)
1 tablespoon maple syrup
1 tablespoon molasses
1 tablespoon Worcestershire sauce
1 tablespoon Dijon mustard
1 tablespoon brown sugar
1 teaspoon ground cumin
250 g (8 oz) tomatoes, chopped
1 quantity of pickled okra (p.164)

method

To make the baked beans, drain haricots from water. Preheat oven to 180°C (350°F). Sauté onion and garlic in a little olive oil. Add all other ingredients and bring to simmer on stove top. Cover with foil and bake in oven for 1½ hours, or until beans are tender.

For the hocks place all ingredients except the hocks, mustard and sugar in a pot with 2 litres (2½ pints) of water. Bring to the boil, skim and reduce to a simmer. Place hocks in this court bouillon and bring back to a gentle simmer. Cook until the bone is able to be twisted but the flesh is still firm but tender, approximately 1 hour. Remove from liquid and cool. Reduce stock by half. Remove skin from hock.

To finish individually, as in my restaurant, place a hock in a black iron pan with 250 ml (8 fl oz) of reduced stock and cover with foil. Put in a hot oven (200°C/400°F) to reheat. Remove hock to a tray and continue reducing stock to a sauce consistency. Brush hock with the thinned mustard then sprinkle hock liberally with brown sugar and caramelise under a very hot grill. Plate hock and drizzle with sauce. Place spicy baked beans next to hock and garnish with pickled okra.

SPICY, SWEET FRUIT SHIRAZ, POSSIBLY BLENDED WITH SOME GRENACHE. THIS IS A DECADENT DISH AND CALLS FOR A HEDONISTIC STYLE OF WINE. OLD-VINE SHIRAZ PROVIDES THE GREATEST CONCENTRATION OF SPICY FLAVOURS. THE STYLE OF WINE WOULD SWAMP MOST OTHER DISHES BUT MEETS ITS PERFECT MATCH AS THIS DISH IS A COMPLEX BLEND OF SMOKY, SWEET AND SOUR FLAVOURS.

70. LITTLE PAVS WITH CLOTTED CREAM, WILD STRAWBERRIES & ROSE SYRUP

ingredients

8 egg whites
300 g (10 oz) castor sugar
¼ teaspoon vanilla extract
¼ teaspoon water
¼ teaspoon bicarbonate of soda
¼ teaspoon vinegar
400 ml (13 fl oz) pure cream (at least 45% fat content)
extra 150 g (5 oz) sugar
handful rose petals
200 g (6½ oz) wild or alpine strawberries

method

Beat egg whites until they begin to hold their shape (I find it easiest to use an electric beater to make pavlova). Add half the castor sugar and beat for 3 minutes on high speed. Add the remaining sugar and beat for a further 5 minutes at high speed. Combine the vanilla, water, bicarbonate of soda and vinegar and incorporate into the meringue.

Cut strips of baking paper 5 cm wide by 20 cm long (2 in x 8 in). Form these rectangles into rings and tape ends together. Pipe or spoon meringue into the 'collars' on a baking sheet and cook at 100°C (200°F) for 2 hours and then reduce to 70°C (150°F) for a further hour. Cool and store in a sealed container at room temperature.

Bring cream to the boil in a small pan, simmer for 3–4 minutes and pour into a non-corrosive tray. Leave for 3 hours to cool and set properly.

Place the sugar and the rose petals in a heavy small saucepan and add 250 ml (8 fl oz) water. Bring to the boil and simmer for about 10 minutes, reducing to a light syrup. Cool.

Spoon clotted cream on each meringue. Top this with a generous amount of wild strawberries and drizzle over a small amount of rose syrup.

DEMI-SEC SPARKLING WINE. THE STRAWBERRIES ARE MUCH MORE FRAGRANT AND DELICATE IN FLAVOUR THAN THEIR LARGER COUSINS, SO THE APPROPRIATE WINE TO MATCH THE DISH SHOULD SHOWCASE THIS FRAGRANCE AND NOT SWAMP IT WITH OVERLY RICH AND LUSCIOUS CHARACTERS.

73. FIG & RASPBERRY TART WITH TOASTED ALMOND ICE-CREAM

71. GRATINEE OF MIXED BERRIES WITH A SABAYON

ingredients

125 g (4 oz) raspberries
125 g (4 oz) strawberries
125 g (4 oz) blueberries
125 g (4 oz) blackberries
4 egg yolks
4 tablespoons sugar
200 ml (6½ fl oz) demi-sec sparkling wine (Domaine Chandon cuvée riche where available)

method

Mix berries in a large bowl and divide between 4 serving plates.

In a copper bowl mix yolks, sugar and wine. Place bowl directly over low heat and whisk until soft peaks form, mixture holds its own shape and there is no liquid left at the bottom of the bowl. If you don't have a copper bowl, do this in a stainless steel bowl set over a saucepan of simmering water, making sure that the water does not come into contact with the bowl.

Spoon sabayon mixture over the berries and toast the top to a golden brown colour under a very hot grill. Serve immediately.

DEMI-SEC SPARKLING WINE. IT IS ALWAYS CORRECT TO DRINK THE SAME WINE YOU COOK WITH, OR AT LEAST THE SAME STYLE OF WINE. THE SPARKLING DEMI-SEC IS NOT A CHEAP WINE, HOWEVER IT DOES ADD JUST THAT EXTRA DIMENSION TO THE SABAYON. THE FRUIT FLAVOUR IS REDOLENT OF BERRIES, PARTICULARLY ON THE BOUQUET, AND ITS LIGHT TINGLING FINISH WOULD ALSO COUNTERBALANCE THE CREAMY AND EGGY NATURE OF THE SABAYON.

72. BANANA & FRANGIPANE CREAM PIZZA WITH HONEY ICE-CREAM

ingredients

6 egg yolks
180 ml (6 fl oz) honey
250 ml (8 fl oz) cream
250 ml (8 fl oz) milk
100 g (3½ oz) ground almonds
200 ml (6½ fl oz) pastry cream (p.162)
1 tablespoon kirsch
300 g (10 oz) puff pastry
4 bananas
90 g (3 oz) icing sugar

method

Whisk the egg yolks and honey in a bowl until incorporated. Combine the cream and milk in a saucepan. Bring to the boil and add to the egg yolk mixture. Return the mixture to the saucepan and cook over low heat, stirring constantly, until the mixture coats the back of a spoon. Cool over iced water, strain and churn in an ice-cream machine according to the manufacturer's instructions.

Combine ground almonds, pastry cream and kirsch in a bowl and mix.

Roll out the puff pastry on a lightly floured bench and cut 4 rounds, each of about 12 cm (5 in). Place on a non-stick baking tray and refrigerate for 15 minutes.

Preheat oven to 250°C (480°F). Remove pastry from refrigerator and spread some pastry cream over each disc to within 1 cm (½ in) of the edges. Peel bananas. Take one banana and slice it on an angle then fan over a base. Repeat the process for each base. Sieve a generous amount of icing sugar over each pizza and bake in oven until pastry is crisp and cooked, and the sugar has glazed the bananas (about 10–12 minutes). Plate up and serve with a scoop of honey ice-cream.

BOTRYTIS-AFFECTED SEMILLON. SELECT A MEDIUM RICH WINE THAT STILL HAS PLENTY OF ACID AT THE FINISH. THE MARMALADE AND APRICOT FLAVOURS WILL SIT WELL WITH THE FRUIT AND FLORAL CHARACTER OF THE TOPPING. THE HIGH ACID FINISH WILL BALANCE THE CREAMY TEXTURE OF THE FRANGIPANE CREAM AND THE ICE-CREAM.

73. FIG & RASPBERRY TART WITH TOASTED ALMOND ICE-CREAM

ingredients

8 ripe but firm figs
250 g (8 oz) raspberries
2 eggs
110 g (3 oz) castor sugar
150 ml (5 fl oz) heavy cream

pastry

250 g (8 oz) flour
2 tablespoons castor sugar
¼ teaspoon salt
¼ teaspoon grated lemon rind
250 g (8 oz) unsalted butter
2 tablespoons water
1 teaspoon vanilla extract

ice-cream

155 g (5 oz) almonds
500 ml (16 fl oz) heavy cream
500 ml (16 fl oz) milk
12 egg yolks
110 g (3½ oz) sugar

RICH BOTRYTISED SEMILLON, PERHAPS BLENDED WITH SAUVIGNON BLANC THAT HAS BEEN AGED IN OAK. THE APRICOT AND MARMALADE CHARACTERS OF THE BOTRYTIS ARE IDEAL PARTNERS FOR THE FRUIT COMPONENT, WHILST THE OAK MATURATION ADDS A LAYER OF NUTTY AND TOFFEE FLAVOURS THAT WILL ENHANCE THE ICE-CREAM.

method

First make the ice-cream. Place almonds on a baking dish and toast under a hot grill or in an oven until golden brown. On a chopping board, roughly chop the toasted almonds. Place the cream, milk and chopped almonds in a saucepan and bring to the boil. Cream the egg yolks and sugar together in a bowl. Whisk hot milk into egg mixture. Cook over a double boiler until the mixture coats the back of a spoon. Cool quickly over iced water. Churn in an ice-cream machine to the maker's instructions.

To make the pastry, mix together the flour, sugar, salt and lemon rind in a large bowl. Cut the butter into small cubes and, using your hands, rub the butter into the flour mixture. When fully mixed, add a little water and the vanilla extract and mix to form a dough. Do not overmix or the pastry will toughen.

Preheat oven to 160°C (315°F). Roll out pastry on a lightly dusted bench and use it to line a 25–30 cm (10–12 in) tart case. Weight pastry and blind bake for about 25 minutes.

Increase oven temperature to 200°C (400°F). Cut figs in half if they are small or quarters if they are large. Arrange around the prebaked tart shell, cut side up. Sprinkle the raspberries evenly around as well. In a bowl, whisk the eggs and sugar until sugar is dissolved. Add the cream and mix in well. Pour this batter over the figs and raspberries and bake in oven until filling is set.

Cool and serve with toasted almond ice-cream.

74. BLACKBERRY SHORTCAKE WITH LEMON CREAM

ingredients

1 quantity sweet pastry (p.162)
1 quantity pastry cream (p.162)
3 lemons
100 ml (3½ fl oz) cream
450 g (14 oz) blackberries
50 g (1½ oz) sugar
icing sugar for dusting

method

Remove sweet pastry from the refrigerator and, when close to room temperature, roll out on a lightly floured bench to a thickness of 4 mm (⅛ in). Cut out 12 circles, each approximately 6 cm (2½ in), with a pastry cutter. Place on a baking tray and return to the refrigerator for 15 minutes.

Preheat oven to 160°C (315°F). Bake biscuits for 15 minutes and then cool on a cake rack.

Whisk the pastry cream in a bowl to loosen. Grate lemons finely and add rind to pastry cream. In a separate bowl, whip the cream and add this to the pastry cream, gently folding until incorporated.

Take half the blackberries and place in a saucepan with the sugar. Cook over a low heat, crushing the blackberries with the back of a spoon as they warm. Bring to the boil, then purée in a food processor. Pass through a sieve and cool.

On each of 4 serving plates, place a biscuit. On the centre of each, place a dob of lemon cream and surround with blackberries. Pour 2 teaspoons blackberry sauce on each dob of lemon cream. Sauce should run out between the berries a little. Place another biscuit on top of this layer and repeat the process. To finish, top each with a biscuit that has been dusted with icing sugar.

LIGHTER-STYLE, LATE-PICKED RIESLING WITH A FAIR AMOUNT OF ACID. AVOID ANY DESSERT WINES WITH OAK MATURATION AS THE CHARACTER WILL CLASH WITH BOTH THE FRUIT FLAVOUR OF THE BLACKBERRY AND THE LEMON, WHEREAS THE CITRUS-LIKE FRUIT OF RIESLING WILL MATCH WITH BOTH THESE FLAVOURS.

74. BLACKBERRY SHORTCAKE WITH LEMON CREAM

75. HOT BLOOD PLUM SOUFFLÉ WITH BLOOD PLUM ICE-CREAM

75. HOT BLOOD PLUM SOUFFLÉ WITH BLOOD PLUM ICE-CREAM

ingredients

600 g (1¼ lb) blood plums
475 g (15 oz) castor sugar
250 ml (8 fl oz) milk
250 ml (8 fl oz) cream
6 eggs
2 teaspoons pastry cream (p.162)
1 tablespoon unsalted butter

EAU DE VIE MADE FROM PLUMS, OR ICY-COLD SLIVOVITZ. IF YOU GO FOR THE EAU DE VIE YOU'LL GET THE FULL EFFECT OF THE PLUM FLAVOUR, AS IT HAS THE ESSENCE OF PLUM ON THE NOSE AND THE SEARING ALCOHOLIC BURN IN THE AFTERTASTE. SERVING IT VERY COLD CREATES A BALANCE BETWEEN THE TEMPERATURE VERSUS THE ALCOHOL.

method

Score the skins of the blood plums and immerse in a pot of boiling water for about 30 seconds until they start to blister. Remove from water and peel. Discard the skins and place the pulp in a non-corrosive saucepan with 100 g (3½ oz) of the sugar. Simmer gently to reduce all liquid from the plums and remove stones. The plums should have a jammy consistency, and have yielded about 500 ml (16 fl oz). Allow to cool.

Place milk and cream together in a saucepan and bring to the boil. While coming to the boil, separate the eggs, reserve the whites and place the yolks in a bowl with 175 g castor sugar. Cream together and then add the scalded milk/cream mixture a little at a time, whisking between additions. Place the bowl over a double boiler and gently heat whilst continually stirring with a wooden spoon, until the custard thickens and coats the back of the spoon. Cool quickly over iced water and stir in half the stewed plums. Churn in an ice-cream machine, according to the maker's directions.

Preheat oven to 200ºC (400ºF). Mix rest of plums in a copper* or stainless steel bowl with the pastry cream. Reheat gently. While doing this, beat the reserved egg whites (with an electric mixer is best). Once they start to hold their shape, add 200 g (6½ oz) castor sugar and beat on the highest speed until sugar is dissolved. Stop beating at this point or soufflé will have a rubbery texture when cooked.

Remove the plum mixture from the heat as soon as it starts to bubble and fold the meringue through. Spoon resulting mixture into 4 soufflé cups that have been pre-buttered and dusted with sugar. Tidy up the soufflés by running the rims of the cups between your thumb and index finger.

Bake in oven for approximately 8–10 minutes, until the soufflés have risen to their maximum height. Remove from oven and serve immediately with blood plum ice-cream.

*Copper is a slower conductor of heat than stainless steel and therefore better to use when heating. A copper bowl can be placed directly on a heat source when cooking a sabayon or custard. No double boiler is needed and cooking time will be cut by at least 50 per cent.

76. MANDARIN & CARDAMOM BRÛLÉE

ingredients

100 g (3½ oz) sugar
3 egg yolks
1 whole egg
pinch of salt
180 ml (6 fl oz) milk
350 ml (11 fl oz) pure cream (45% fat)
rind of 3 mandarins
5 cardamom pods
80 g (2½ oz) castor sugar

method

Preheat oven to 150°C (300°F). Beat the 100 g (3½ oz) sugar, egg yolks, whole egg and salt together in a bowl. Place the milk, cream, mandarin peel and cardamom pods in a saucepan and bring to the boil. Add to the egg yolk mixture and let stand until flavours have infused. Strain and pour into brûlée moulds. Stand moulds in a bain marie and cook in the oven for about 45 minutes. Brûlées should be set around the outside and just unset in the centre. Give a gentle shake to test. Cool.

Using a wire sieve, shake a little castor sugar over a brûlée. This will disperse the sugar evenly and not result in any unevenness in this layer. Carefully caramelise the sugar under a very hot grill. Allow to harden and serve.

BOTRYTISED-AFFECTED RIESLING. THE CITRUS FLAVOURS OF RIESLING WILL SUIT THE FLAVOUR OF THE CUSTARD, WHILST THE RICH MARMALADE CHARACTER OF THE BOTRYTIS WILL SUIT THE BITTERNESS OF THE BURNT SUGAR. THE WINE SHOULD BE QUITE ACIDIC AT THE FINISH TO CUT THROUGH THE CREAMINESS OF THE CUSTARD.

77. CARAMELISED PEAR PIZZA WITH MASCARPONE

ingredients

100 g (3½ oz) sugar
100 g (3½ oz) unsalted butter
4 firm pears, peeled and sliced
100 ml (3½ fl oz) water
200 g (6½ oz) puff pastry
150 g (5 oz) mascarpone

method

Preheat oven to 200°C (400°F). In a large frypan, heat the sugar and butter together. Shake the pan as the sugar starts to colour, to avoid burning in spots. When mixture is fully caramelised, remove from heat and add pear slices. Toss and return to heat, adding the water to stop further caramelisation or possible burning. Continue cooking the pears for about 5 minutes, until they are softened and the liquid is syrupy. Put pears in a bowl, reserving syrup, and cool.

Roll out puff pastry to a thickness of 4 mm (¼ in). Cut into rounds of diameter about 10–12 cm (4–5 in) using an inverted saucer or pastry cutter. Place pastry discs on a non-stick baking tray and arrange pear slices in an overlapping fashion on each, to a distance of 5 mm (¼ in) from the edge of the pastry. Brush pears liberally with the cooking syrup.

Bake in oven for approximately 8–10 minutes, or until the pastry is browned and cooked. Place a pear pizza on each plate and put a dessertspoon of mascarpone on the centre of each. A little more of the cooking syrup can be drizzled over, if desired.

QUITE SWEET, BOTRYTIS-AFFECTED CHENIN BLANC, WITH PLENTY OF ACID AT THE FINISH. THE FLAVOUR OF CHENIN BLANC IS SOMEWHERE BETWEEN APPLES AND PEARS. A TOUCH OF BOTRYTIS WILL MARRY IN WELL WITH THE CARAMELISED SUGAR, WHILST THE ACID IS NECESSARY TO CUT THROUGH THE PASTRY AND CREAMY TEXTURE OF THE MASCARPONE.

78. PROFITEROLES WITH PISTACHIO ICE-CREAM & HOT MOCHA SAUCE

ingredients

choux pastry
65 ml (2 fl oz) milk
65 ml (2 fl oz) water
½ teaspoon sugar
¼ teaspoon salt
50 g (1½ oz) unsalted butter
70 g (2 oz) flour
3 eggs

ice-cream
150 g (5 oz) pistachio nuts
250 ml (8 fl oz) milk
250 ml (8 fl oz) cream
6 egg yolks
160 g (5 oz) sugar

method

To make the ice-cream, first dry toast the pistachio nuts without colouring - just to develop the nutty flavours slightly. This should take only 3–4 minutes in a heavy pan. Place in a food processor and chop very fine; almost to a meal. In a saucepan, mix the milk, cream and finely chopped nuts and bring to the boil. Whilst this is heating up, cream the egg yolks and sugar together in a bowl. Add the scalded cream and pistachio mixture to this bowl, a little at first, mix, then the rest. Return bowl to low heat and very carefully cook the mixture, stirring, until it thickens slightly, being careful not to scramble the mixture by heating too much. It may be advisable to do this over a double boiler. When thickened, cool over iced water and strain. Churn according to your machine's instructions.

For profiteroles, preheat oven to 220°C (430°F). Place the milk and water in a saucepan and add the sugar, salt and butter. Bring slowly to the boil and remove from heat. Add all the flour at once and beat with a wooden spoon. Return to a low heat and continue to mix with a wooden spoon until dough stops sticking to the side of the saucepan. Remove dough to the bowl of an electric mixer. On a low–medium speed, incorporate an egg at a time until the dough is smooth.

On a non-stick baking sheet, either pipe or spoon small round pats of dough: the mixture will make at least a dozen. Bake for 15 minutes and then turn oven down to 190°C (375°F) for a further 10 minutes. Store in an airtight container until needed.

To serve, cut profiteroles in half and put 3 halves on each plate. Fill profiterole shells with a small scoop of pistachio ice-cream, and replace top of profiteroles. Pour over mocha sauce.

RICH, LUSCIOUS FORTIFIED MUSCAT. CHOCOLATE IS VERY DIFFICULT TO MATCH WITH WINE, DUE TO ITS INTENSITY OF FLAVOUR AND BITTERSWEET NATURE. FORTIFIED MUSCAT HAS ENOUGH DEPTH OF FLAVOUR TO COPE WITH THIS INTENSITY AND NOT TO BE OVERPOWERED. A MUSCAT WITH A FAIR BIT OF AGED MATERIAL INCLUDED IN THE BLEND WOULD BE IDEAL TO MATCH THE NUTTINESS OF THE ICE-CREAM.

79. WHITE CHOCOLATE & DRIED BLUEBERRY ICE-CREAM 'KREEM BETWEEN'

77. CARAMELISED PEAR PIZZA WITH MASCARPONE

79. WHITE CHOCOLATE & DRIED BLUEBERRY ICE-CREAM 'KREEM BETWEEN'

ingredients

biscuit

125 g (4 oz) butter
¼ teaspoon vanilla extract
50 g (1½ oz) sugar
250 g (8 oz) flour
90 g (3 oz) cornflour
125 g (4 oz) chocolate bits

ice-cream

200 g (6½ oz) blueberries
250 ml (8 fl oz) milk
250 ml (8 fl oz) cream
125 g (4 oz) sugar
5 egg yolks
100 g (3½ oz) white chocolate

1 quantity raspberry sauce (p.167)

method

Cream butter, vanilla and sugar together. Mix flour and cornflour and fold into butter to form a dough. Add chocolate bits. Roll out to 3-mm (⅛-in) thickness. Cut biscuits to desired shape. Place on a tray lined with greaseproof paper and refrigerate for 15 minutes then bake at 160°C (315°F) till firm but not coloured. Cool on a wire cake rack and store in an airtight container until needed.

Place a sheet of baking paper on a baking tray. Spread the blueberries out evenly and put in an oven at 60°C (140°F), or if it is a gas oven with just a pilot light on. For some reason unknown to me, blueberries the same size dry at very different rates. For this reason you must keep a constant check on them, and remove them from the oven one by one as they become sultana-like. Check them every half-hour. Do not over-dry them or they will develop the texture of juniper berries. Store in an airtight container until required.

Place milk and cream in a saucepan and bring to the boil. At the same time put eggs and sugar in a bowl and whisk thoroughly. Pour milk/cream mixture over egg/sugar mixture. Add white chocolate and cook, stirring, in top of double boiler until the custard coats the back of a spoon. Cool immediately over iced water. Churn in an ice-cream machine according to the manufacturer's instructions. When churned place in a bucket and stir in dried blueberries. Because of the high fat content in the white chocolate, allow 3 hours' freezer time before serving.

To serve, place some raspberry sauce on each plate. Put a biscuit in the middle, then 2 scoops of ice-cream on the biscuit and place another biscuit on top.

LIGHTLY FORTIFIED MUSCAT THAT STILL RETAINS ITS FRESH, FRUITY CHARACTER. THE FRAGRANT STYLE HAS ENOUGH LIFT ON THE NOSE AND FRONT PALATE TO MATCH THE FRAGRANCE OF THE BLUEBERRIES, YET ALSO HAS ENOUGH DEPTH OF FLAVOUR TO COPE WITH THE BITTERSWEET FLAVOUR OF THE COOKIES.

80. HOT BUTTER WAFFLES WITH GRILLED PEACHES, VANILLA BEAN ICE-CREAM & RASPBERRY SAUCE

ingredients

4 peaches
50 g (1½ oz) unsalted butter, melted
1 quantity raspberry sauce (p.167)

ice-cream
250 ml (8 fl oz) milk
250 ml (8 fl oz) cream
¼ vanilla bean, split lengthways
6 egg yolks
60 g (2 oz) castor sugar

waffles
75g (2½ oz) sliced almonds
125 g (4 oz) flour
2 teaspoons baking powder
¼ teaspoon bicarbonate of soda
2 tablespoons sugar
3 eggs, separated
250 ml (8 fl oz) milk
125 ml (4 fl oz) crème fraiche
50 ml (1½ fl oz) unsalted butter, melted
1 tablespoon warm honey

method

To make ice-cream, place milk, cream and vanilla bean in a saucepan and bring to the boil. At the same time, put egg yolks and sugar in a bowl and whisk together until creamed. Add a quarter of the milk/cream mixture to the yolks and mix. Then add the rest and mix in. In the top of a double boiler, cook the custard, stirring constantly, until it thickens and coats the back of a wooden spoon. Remove from heat immediately and cool over iced water. Churn in ice-cream machine according to the manufacturer's instructions.

For the waffles, dry toast the almonds lightly in a heavy pan or oven and place in a food processor. Run motor and turn into a meal. Add the flour, baking powder, bicarbonate of soda and sugar. Transfer mixture to a bowl.

In a separate bowl combine the yolks, milk, crème fraiche, melted butter and honey. Add to the dry ingredients and mix until just incorporated. Beat the egg whites until soft peaks form and fold through the batter.

Peel the peaches by immersing them in boiling water for 10 seconds, then cooling in iced water. The skin should just about fall off if the peaches are correctly ripe. Cut peaches in half, take out the stones, and cut in half again. Brush peaches with a little melted butter and grill.

Cook waffle batter in waffle iron according to the manufacturer's directions. Top with grilled peaches, raspberry sauce and vanilla bean ice-cream.

MEDIUM-SWEET SEMILLON, WHERE THE SWEETNESS COMES FROM THE NATURALLY RIPE GRAPES AND NOT BOTRYTIS. THIS DISH DOES NOT REQUIRE AN OVERLY RICH WINE AS THERE ARE PLENTY OF RICH FLAVOURS AND TEXTURES IN IT. THE WINE SHOULD HAVE THE FRUIT FLAVOUR TO COMPLEMENT THE PEACHES AND A LIGHTNESS IN THE MID PALATE AND FINISH TO PREVENT THE COMBINATION BEING CLOYING.

81. BREAD & BUTTER PUDDING

ingredients

100 g (3½ oz) raisins
50 ml (1½ fl oz) amaretto
1 loaf of brioche (p.160)
100 g (3½ oz) unsalted butter, softened
100 g (3½ oz) apricot jam
400 ml (13 fl oz) milk
400 ml (13 fl oz) cream
½ vanilla bean, split lengthways
7 eggs
100 g (3½ oz) castor sugar
150 ml (5 fl oz) cream

method

Place raisins in a bowl and pour over warmed amaretto. Leave to soak overnight.

Take the crusts off the loaf of brioche and slice it 1 cm (½ in) thick. Spread each slice with a film of unsalted butter and then a thin layer of apricot jam. Cut each slice into quarters.

Spread three-quarters of the macerated raisins on the bottom of a baking dish. Layer the triangles of brioche over the raisins in an overlapping fashion. Sprinkle the remaining raisins over the top of the brioche.

In a bowl, combine the eggs and sugar and whisk until they are creamed. Bring the milk, cream and vanilla bean together to the boil and whisk into the egg mixture. Strain and pour into the baking tray over the brioche and let stand for 15 minutes.

Preheat oven to 150°C (300°F). Put in a water bath and bake for 1 hour. Finally, put dish under a hot grill and 'toast' until the edges of the brioche are golden brown and crisp.

Serve warm with running cream.

THERE ARE TWO OPTIONS HERE. FIRST, A COMPLEX BOTRYTIS-AFFECTED SEMILLON, POSSIBLY BLENDED WITH SAUVIGNON BLANC. THIS WILL HAVE ALL THE RICH TOFFEE FLAVOURS TO MATCH THE DECADENT, CREAMY CUSTARD. THE OTHER IS A NUT-BASED LIQUEUR THAT WILL REINFORCE THE RAISINS THAT HAVE BEEN SOAKED IN AMARETTO.

82. POONIE'S ICKY STICKY DATE & CHOCOLATE PUDDING WITH BUTTERSCOTCH SAUCE

ingredients

430 g (14 oz) brown sugar
240 g (8 oz) unsalted butter
250 g (8 fl oz) cream
175 g (6 oz) dates
1 teaspoon bicarbonate of soda
300 ml (10 fl oz) boiling water
60 g (2 fl oz) unsalted butter
extra 100 g (3½ oz) brown sugar
1 teaspoon vanilla extract
1 egg
230 g (7 oz) plain flour
1½ teaspoons baking powder
150 g (5 oz) bittersweet chocolate

method

Boil the first 3 ingredients together for 5 minutes, or until mixture starts to go brown and thicken slightly. Pour half of this sauce into a 20 cm (8 in) springform tin that has first been lined with buttered aluminium foil. Reserve rest of sauce.

Preheat oven to 175ºC (350ºF). Pit the dates and place in a bowl with the bicarbonate of soda. Pour over the boiling water and allow to cool. Combine the butter, extra sugar and vanilla extract and beat with an electric mixer until the mixture is creamed. Add the egg and then stir in the date mixture. Mix together the flour and baking powder and fold through until everything is evenly incorporated. Roughly chop the chocolate and stir through. Pour into the lined tin and bake for 30 minutes, then decrease oven temperature to 160ºC (315ºF) and cook a further 60 minutes.

Test by inserting a small knife to see if totally cooked. Serve piping hot with reserved butterscotch sauce.

RICH, FORTIFIED MUSCADELLE, TYPICALLY CALLED LIQUEUR TOKAY. THESE WINES ARE INCREDIBLY CONCENTRATED AND DEVELOP TOFFEE, CARAMEL AND MOLASSES FLAVOURS THAT SIT PERFECTLY WITH THIS RICH DESSERT. THE LITTLE HEAT AT THE FINISH OF THIS WINE WILL HELP BALANCE ALL THE SWEETNESS IN THE DISH.

81. BREAD & BUTTER PUDDING

BLAKES BASICS

CHICKEN STOCK

ingredients

1 kg (2 lb) chicken bones
100 g (3½ oz) carrots
1 onion
1 stick celery
1 leek
1 clove garlic
1 teaspoon white peppercorns
2 bay leaves
4 sprigs thyme

method

Wash the chicken bones under running cold water for 30 minutes. Put in a large saucepan or small stockpot. Wash the carrots, onion, celery and leek. Rough chop and add to the chicken bones. Flatten the garlic with the side of a cook's knife and add to the stockpot along with the peppercorns, bay leaves and thyme. Cover ingredients with 4 litres (6½ pints) water and bring to a boil. Simmer for 3–4 hours, skimming every so often to remove any fat or scum. Strain and cool completely before refrigerating.

VEAL STOCK

ingredients

2 kg (4 lb) veal bones
1 calf's foot or pig's trotter
2 onions
200 g (6½ oz) carrots
2 sticks celery
100 g (3½ oz) mushrooms
3 cloves garlic
500 ml (16 fl oz) red wine
5 over-ripe tomatoes
1 teaspoon white peppercorns
4 bay leaves
6 sprigs thyme

method

Preheat oven to 220°C (450°F). Roughly chop the veal bones and roast in the oven until lightly browned. Remove bones from the roasting pan and put in a very large stockpot with the calf's foot or trotter. Drain fat from the roasting pan and add the onions, carrots, celery, mushrooms and garlic. Lightly roast the vegetables in the oven until golden in colour. Add red wine and scrape off anything that may have stuck to the roasting tray.

Pour the contents of the roasting tray into the stockpot. Add the tomatoes, peppercorns, bay leaves and thyme. Add 10 litres (16 pints) water and bring to the boil. Simmer and skim. Continue simmering for 8 hours, skimming when any fat or scum rises to the surface. Top up with cold water when necessary.

Strain the stock through a fine-mesh sieve. Return strained veal stock to the stockpot or saucepan and reduce to the strength required.

DEMI-GLAZE

ingredients

3 litres (5 pints) veal stock (p.158)

method

Reduce veal stock over medium heat until it becomes viscous and shiny. Should yield about 1–1.5 litres (1½–2½ pints) of demi-glaze.

MAYONNAISE

ingredients

3 egg yolks
2 teaspoons white wine vinegar
2 teaspoons Dijon mustard
200 ml (6½ fl oz) olive oil
200 ml (6½ fl oz) vegetable oil
salt and freshly ground white pepper

method

Whisk together the yolks, vinegar and mustard in a bowl. In a slow, steady stream, add the oils while continually whisking. When oils are completely incorporated, whisk in 2 tablespoons warm water to help stabilise the mayonnaise. Season with salt and freshly ground white pepper.

CAESAR DRESSING

ingredients

2 eggs
1 clove garlic
2 tablespoons Worcestershire sauce
2 teaspoons Dijon mustard
2 anchovies
50 ml (1½ fl oz) white wine vinegar
100 ml (3½ fl oz) olive oil
100 ml (3½ fl oz) vegetable oil

method

In a food processor, combine all the ingredients except for the oils. Blend until smooth. Gradually add the oils in a steady stream until fully incorporated and mixture is a mayonnaise consistency. Season.

BRIOCHE

ingredients

450 g (14 oz) unsalted butter
3 teaspoons fresh yeast
2 teaspoons tepid water
2 teaspoons salt
2 tablespoons sugar
1½ tablespoons milk
470 g (15 oz) flour
6 eggs

method

Take the butter out of the refrigerator 20 minutes before starting the dough. Dissolve the yeast in the tepid water. In another bowl dissolve the salt and sugar in the milk. In the bowl of an electric mixer with a dough-hook attachment, place the salt/sugar/milk mixture. On a low speed, add the flour, then the yeast solution. Beat for 2 minutes, then add 4 eggs all at once, continuing to beat until the dough is smooth. Add the remaining eggs 1 at a time. Increase to medium speed and continue to beat for another 10 minutes. Lower the speed of the machine and add the butter in small chunks. Mix until completely incorporated.

Place the dough in a large bowl, cover with a cloth and leave standing to rise for 2 hours at room temperature. When dough has doubled in bulk, knock the dough back. Cover, place in the refrigerator for another 2 hours until it has once again doubled in size. Knock the dough back again and refrigerate overnight. (Dough may be kept refrigerated for a week at this stage, or when baked a loaf will freeze well for a month if well wrapped.)

To cook in a tin loaf form, shape some of the brioche dough into a couple of balls. Lay these balls along the bottom of a buttered tin loaf and allow them to rise for 2 hours to double in size. Each ball should blend into the next one and have risen to near the top of the tin. Preheat oven to 200°C (400°F). Brush dough with beaten egg and bake in oven for 30–35 minutes until golden brown.

BASIL BREAD

ingredients

600 ml (18 fl oz) tepid water
30 g (1 oz) fresh yeast
1 kg (2 lb) flour
75 g (2½ oz) sugar
30 g (1 oz) salt
1 bunch basil, leaves chopped
1 egg, beaten

method

Preheat oven to 240°C (465°F). Put the water and yeast in the bowl of an electric mixer and whisk together. Using the dough-hook attachment, with the motor on low speed, add the flour, sugar, salt and roughly chopped basil. Mix until a smooth dough forms. Cover with a damp tea towel and leave to prove in a warm spot in the kitchen. When the dough has doubled in size, gently knock back without overworking.

Shape the dough to whatever shape you require and allow to prove on a baking sheet or in a mould for about 60 minutes, covering while you do so to avoid drying out.

Brush the dough with the beaten egg and bake for 35–45 minutes, depending upon its shape and size.

PASTA DOUGH

ingredients

250 g (8 oz) flour
1 teaspoon salt
3 eggs
2 tablespoons olive oil

method

Place flour and salt in the workbowl of a food processor. With motor running, add the eggs one by one, finishing with the olive oil. Stop motor as soon as incorporated. Turn out mixture onto a workbench and knead into a dough. Wrap in plastic wrap and rest for 10 minutes.

PIZZA DOUGH

ingredients

100 ml (3½ fl oz) warm water
1 teaspoon dry yeast
½ tablespoon honey
125 g (4 oz) flour
60 g (2 oz) semolina
½ teaspoon salt
1 tablespoon olive oil

method

Mix the warm water, yeast and honey together to activate the yeast. If the water is not warm, the yeast will not activate, and if the water is too hot, the yeast will die. Place flour, semolina and salt in the workbowl of a food processor. Turn motor on and add the olive oil and then the yeast mixture in a steady stream. A dough should start to form. Turn out onto a workbench and knead for a few minutes to develop the gluten in the flour. Place in a lightly oiled bowl, cover with a damp tea towel and place in a warm part of the kitchen to double in size.

When it has, knock it back and divide into 4 equal parts. Roll each under the palm of your hand to redevelop the elasticity in the dough. Dough is now ready to make individual pizzas; recombine dough to make a single, large pizza.

SHORTCRUST PASTRY

ingredients

180 g (6 oz) unsalted butter
1 egg
4 tablespoons water
250 g (8 oz) flour
pinch of salt

method

Beat the butter until it is light and creamy (easiest in an electric mixer with the paddle attachment). Add the egg and then the water. Sift the flour on to a workbench, add a pinch of salt and make a well in the centre. Place the creamed butter in this well. Using your fingers, gradually incorporate the flour into the butter to form a dough. Do not overwork or the gluten in the flour will toughen the dough. Wrap in plastic wrap and refrigerate for 1 hour before use.

SWEET PASTRY

ingredients

120 g (4 oz) unsalted butter
120 g (4 oz) castor sugar
2 eggs
300 g (10 oz) flour
pinch of salt

method

Cream the butter and sugar with an electric beater. Add 1 egg, incorporate, then the other.

Mix the flour and salt on a workbench, and form a well in the centre. Put the creamed butter mixture in the well and mix with your hands until a smooth dough forms. A little water may be added if dough is dry.

PASTRY CREAM

ingredients

250 ml (8 fl oz) milk
¼ vanilla bean, split lengthways
3 egg yolks
75 g (2½ oz) sugar
2 tablespoons flour
25 g (¾ oz) unsalted butter

method

Place the milk and vanilla bean in a saucepan and bring to the boil. Put egg yolks and sugar in a bowl and whisk to dissolve sugar. Add flour and whisk in well. When milk has boiled, strain to remove vanilla bean, then stir a couple of tablespoons into the egg yolk mixture and incorporate. Add half the remaining milk and mix in completely before adding the rest. Pour back into saucepan and return to the stove. Bring back to the boil while continually whisking and then remove from the heat after 30 seconds. Stir in unsalted butter and pour into a container. Cool, cover and refrigerate.

PRESERVED LEMONS

ingredients

12 lemons
500 g (1 lb) rocksalt
1 sterilised preserving jar

method

Juice 6 of the lemons. Stand the other 6 on their ends and, with a sharp knife, cut into quarters lengthways – but not all the way through: leave the last 1 cm (½ in) intact to hold the lemons together.

Put the rocksalt in a bowl. Holding a lemon in one hand over the rocksalt, pack the salt tightly into the centre of the lemon with the other hand. Place lemon in preserving jar. Repeat the process on each lemon, packing them into the glass jar as tightly as possible. Completely cover with lemon juice and store in a pantry for 1 month before using.

The size of the jar will determine how many lemons can be preserved. The jar has to be packed tightly.

TOMATO SAUCE

ingredients

½ *small onion*
2 cloves garlic
2 tablespoons olive oil
3 over-ripe tomatoes
1 tablespoon tomato paste
5 sprigs thyme

method

Dice onion and garlic very fine and sauté in olive oil to soften. Chop up tomatoes and add to the saucepan, along with the tomato paste and thyme. Cook slowly to reduce all the water out. Remove from heat, purée and pass through a strainer.

TOMATO CONCASSE

method

With a paring knife, score the tomatoes with an 'x' at the opposite end to where the stem was once attached. Immerse tomatoes in boiling water for 10 seconds or until they start to blister. Plunge them into iced water immediately until cold. Peel off the skin and cut in half crossways. Hold the tomato halves cut side down and squeeze to rid them of their seeds and water. Dice to the required size ready for further use.

BEER BATTER

ingredients

250 g (8 oz) plain flour
60 g (2 oz) cornflour
300 ml (10 fl oz) sparkling ale
300 ml (10 fl oz) soda water

method

Place the flours in a large bowl and whisk together. Add the beer and soda water and mix to incorporate. Whisk vigorously to get rid of any lumps. Let stand for 10 minutes and then whisk again for 30 seconds. If for some reason there are still lumps, simply strain them out. The batter will fry crisper if no salt is added and it is not refrigerated.

ROASTED PEPPERS

method

Whether the peppers to be roasted are red, yellow or green, the process is the same. Cut the peppers in quarters lengthways and remove all seeds, core and ribbing. Press down on a tray skin side up. Place under a hot griller until the skins are scorched and blistered. Remove from heat and cover with a tea towel for 5 minutes. The skins should very easily come away from the flesh. Be careful not to over-grill yellow peppers as they will take on a brown tinge from the scorched skin. It may be more advisable to remove the skins of yellow peppers with a sharp vegetable peeler and then slowly braise the flesh in olive oil to obtain a similar texture and flavour to roasting.

PICKLED OKRA

ingredients

100 g okra
200 ml (6½ fl oz) water
100 ml (3½ fl oz) white wine vinegar
40 g (1½ oz) sugar
2 bay leaves
10 peppercorns
1 chilli
1 teaspoon coriander seed
1 teaspoon cumin seed
1 shallot, roughly chopped
1 cinnamon stick

method

Combine all ingredients except for the okra. Bring to the boil and simmer for 10 minutes. Pour over okra and place in sterilised storage jars. Keep for 3–4 days before using.

HUMMUS

ingredients

250 g (8 oz) chickpeas
3 cloves garlic
juice of 3 lemons
150 g (5 oz) tahini
100 ml (3½ fl oz) olive oil

method

To make hummus, soak chickpeas in water for a minimum of 6 hours. After soaking, pour off old water and cover with fresh water. Bring to the boil and simmer, skimming any scum from the cooking process off the top of the water. When tender, drain and place chickpeas in a food processor with garlic, lemon juice and tahini. With motor running, gradually add some water to form a paste of dipping consistency. Add olive oil and cool. When cool, season and add a little more water if hummus thickens too much.

TAPENADE

ingredients

300 g (10 oz) kalamata olives
50 g (1½ oz) capers
50 g (1½ oz) anchovies
30 g (1 oz) chopped Italian parsley
2 cloves garlic, chopped
50 ml (1½ fl oz) extra-virgin olive oil

method

To make tapenade, pit olives and put in a food processor with capers, anchovies, parsley and garlic. Process for 10 seconds, stop and scrape down sides. Pulse until a coarse paste forms. Remove from processor and, in a bowl, incorporate olive oil.

AIOLI

ingredients

4 cloves garlic
2 egg yolks
1 teaspoon Dijon mustard
2 tablespoons white wine vinegar
250 ml (8 fl oz) olive oil

method

To make aioli, place garlic in a small saucepan, cover with water, bring to a boil and simmer for 3 minutes. Drain and place in a food processor with egg yolks, mustard and vinegar. Purèe ingredients and, with motor running, add olive oil in a slow, steady stream. Season.

BEURRE BLANC

ingredients

1 tablespoon white wine
1 tablespoon lemon juice
160 g (5 oz) unsalted butter

method

In a non-corrosive saucepan, heat the white wine and lemon juice together and bring to a gentle simmer. After 30 seconds, remove from the heat and whisk in cold butter a little at a time. You may have to return the saucepan to the heat occasionally to increase heat, but be careful not to overheat as the mixture can separate.

When all the butter has been incorporated, season and put aside in a warm place until coulibiac is ready.

MASALA SAUCE

ingredients

2 teaspoons belacan (shrimp paste)
1 teaspoon szechwan peppercorns
2 teaspoons dried prawns
1 teaspoon cumin seed
2 teaspoons coriander seed
75 ml (2½ fl oz) vegetable oil
1 tablespoon sesame oil
1 brown onion, finely diced
4 cloves garlic, minced
1 tablespoon minced ginger
1 teaspoon minced galangal
5 bird's-eye chillies, minced
4 coriander roots, finely chopped
1 teaspoon turmeric
pinch freshly grated nutmeg
8 fresh curry leaves
1 stick cinnamon
100 ml (3½ fl oz) tomato purée
150 ml (5 fl oz) coconut cream
50 g (1½ oz) palm sugar, shaved
1.5 litres veal stock (p.158)
1 tablespoon fish sauce

method

To make the sauce, first dry-roast the belacan in a heavy-based frying pan over a medium heat for a minute or two. Set aside, then dry-roast the szechwan peppercorns, dried prawns, cumin and coriander together; grind them.

Heat a large, wide-based saucepan, add the oils and fry the onion, garlic, ginger, galangal, chilli and coriander roots until the onions just begin to colour. Add the ground prawn mixture and all the other spices, stirring until the mixture becomes fragrant. Stir in the tomato purée, coconut cream and palm sugar and cook on a gentle heat for a few minutes until the mixture starts to bubble.

Add veal stock to the saucepan, bring to a boil, then reduce the heat and simmer for 1 hour to reduce until the sauce coats the back of a spoon. Skim to remove any excess oil or scum. Remove from heat and strain. Add the fish sauce and adjust the seasoning to taste.

RASPBERRY SAUCE

ingredients

250 g (8 oz) raspberries
100 g (3½ oz) sugar
juice of ½ lemon

method

Combine all ingredients in a non-corrosive saucepan and bring to the boil. Purée, strain and cool. Reduce further if a thicker sauce is required.

MOCHA SAUCE

ingredients

100 g (3½ oz) dark chocolate
50 ml (1½ fl oz) espresso coffee
50 ml (1½ fl oz) milk
1 tablespoon pure cream
1 tablespoon sugar
1 tablespoon unsalted butter

method

For the sauce, melt the chocolate in a double boiler. In a saucepan, bring the espresso coffee, milk and cream to the boil. Remove from the heat, stir in the sugar, then the melted chocolate and lastly the butter.

ACKNOWLEDGEMENTS

Acknowledgements and dedications in books have always struck me as being a little bit clichéd. It's not until you complete a book that you realise that there are people who need to be recognised for their contribution to it. Publisher Sue Hines, art director Grant Slaney and photographer Simon Griffiths are three such people. And, of course, Grant Van Every, who provided the wine notes in this book.

To everybody else who has supported me over the years, thank you.

INDEX

Figures in **bold** indicate photographs

Aioli 165
Almond, ice-cream 138
Apples, sautéd 59
Artichoke, gratinee of
    young 46
    Jerusalem, soup 59
    potato & mascarpone
    pie 68
Asparagus 69
    & fontina tortelli with
    vegetable essence & truffle
    oil 49
    char-grilled 21
Aubergine, *see* eggplant
Avocado 16

Baba ghannouj, smoky 95
Baked beans, spicy 132
    ham hock with spicy baked
    beans & pickled okra 132
'Baked in a bag' chicken breast
    with prosciutto & braised
    witlof 113
Balsamic drizzle 66
Banana & frangipane cream
    pizza with honey ice-cream
    137
Barramundi, steamed wild 110
Basil, bread 160
    risotto 110
    prawn &, ravioli 54
Batter, beer 163
BBQ, fillet of beef with
    gorgonzola polenta & red
    onion jam 122, **116–7**
    king prawns with
    eggplant–haloumi fritters,
    tabouleh & turmeric
    oil 36, **32–3**
    pork, king crab &,
    ricepaper rolls 19
    quail with zucchini fritters
    & thyme hollandaise 83

salmon Nicoise
    salad 40, **44–5**
    tuna steak with a warm
    potato salad & salsa verde
    104, **100–1**
Beans, broad 20
    spicy baked 132
    white, 86 119
Beef, BBQ fillet 122
    peppered ox fillet 120
Beer batter 163
Beetroot dressing 26
    risotto with kangaroo
    prosciutto 76, **80–1**
Berries, mixed, gratinee of 136
Beurre blanc 165
Blackberry shortcake with
    lemon cream 139, **140–1**
Blackened quail with a green
    pawpaw salad 82
Blueberry, dried, white
    chocolate &, ice-cream 152
Bok choy 131
Bread, & butter pudding
    154, **156–7**
    basil 160
    brioche 160
Brioche 160
    crumbs 8
Broad beans 20
Brûlée, mandarin & cardomom
    145
Burger, venison 124
Butter, citrus 47
    pistachio 112
    wasabi 8
Butterscotch sauce 155

Caesar salad dressing 159,
Calf's liver, grilled 95
    parmesan crumbed 103
Caramelised pear pizza with
    mascarpone 146, **150–1**

Cardomom brûlée 145
Carpaccio, tuna 6
Cauliflower soup, chilled 18
Caviar 6, 9
Char-grilled asparagus with
    chopped egg & parmesan oil
    21, **22–3**
    baby octopus on char-
    grilled vegetables with a
    balsamic drizzle 66
Cheese, asparagus & fontina
    tortelli 49
    goat's, fennel & olive tart 27
    gnocchi 130
    gorgonzola 103
    polenta 122
    gruyère toasts 60
Chicken, breast, 'baked in a
    bag' 113
    paillard of 112
    sage-roasted 130
    stock 158
Chickpeas, hummus 164
Chilled cauliflower soup with
    curry cream & shucked
    oysters 18
    roasted tomato soup with
    yabbies & avocado 16
Chilli corn soup with steamed
    clams 58
    mango salsa 74
    mayonnaise 124
    pickled lettuce 7
Chinese cabbage, *see* bok choy
Chips, lattice 34
Chive buerre blanc 67
Chocolate, date &, pudding
    155
    white, & dried blueberry
    ice-cream 152
Chutney, red pepper 123
Citrus butter 47
Clams 69, 58

169

Coconut rice 125
Cod, blue-eye 111
Concasse, tomato 163
Coriander oil 20
    pesto 94
    yoghurt 61
Corn soup, chilli 58
    cakes 35
Coulibiac of atlantic salmon with chive buerre blanc & salmon roe 67, **71–1**
Courgette, *see* zucchini
Couscous, preserved lemon 112
Crab remoulade 41
    mud 46
Cream, clotted 133
    curry 18
    horseradish 34
    lemon 139
    pastry 162
Crisped Sydney rock oysters with chilli pickled lettuce & ginger sauce 7, **12–3**
    zucchini flowers stuffed with goat's cheese ricotta on ratatouille 56, **62–3**
Crisps, eggplant 20
    root 105
Cucumber, pickled 34
    tomato &, salsa 14
Curried dhal soup with seared scallops & coriander yoghurt 61
Curry, cream 18
    red Thai kangaroo 125

Date & chocolate pudding 155
Demi-glaze 159
Dough, pasta 161
    pizza 161
Dressing, balsamic 66
    beet 26

Caesar 159
Duck, & wild mushroom pastie with white bean mash 86
    breast, roast 87
    cakes, grilled 74
    ragout 75
    roast 131

Egg, chopped with asparagus 21
Eggplant, crisps 20
    grilled 89
    haloumi fritters 36
    relish 118
    smoky baba ghannouj 95
Essence, red pepper 110

Fennel, goat's cheese, olive &, tart 27
    shaved, with tuna carpaccio 6
    tomato–, stew 47

Fig & raspberry tart with toasted almond ice-cream **134-5**, 138
Fish, barramundi, steamed wild 110
    BBQ tuna steak 104
    caviar 6, 9
    coulibiac of atlatic salmon 67
    ocean trout gravlax 35
    pistachio crusted blue-eye cod 111
    salmon Nicoise salad 40
    roe 67
    sardine pizza 89
    salt-cured salmon 88
    sardine fillets 47
    smoked salmon stack 34
    tuna carpaccio 6
    mayonnaise 29

    tartare 20
    whole deep-fried baby snapper 105
Fontina, asparagus &, tortelli 49
Frangipane cream, banana &, pizza 137
Fricassée, wild mushroom 102
Fritters, eggplant–haloumi 36
    zucchini 83

Garlic, twice-baked roast, soufflé 39
Gazpacho sauce 38
Ginger sauce 7
Gnocchi, goat's cheese 130
    saffron potato 69
Goat's cheese, gnocchi 130
    ricotta 55
    fennel & olive tart with red pepper sauce 27
Gorgonzola 103
    polenta 122
Gratinee, mixed berries with a sabayon 136
    young artichokes with mud crab & tomato salsa 46
Gravlax, ocean trout 35
Grilled calf's liver & pancetta on pommes sarladaise with smoky baba ghannouj 95
    duck cakes with a chilli–mango salsa 74
Gruyère toasts 60

Ham, hock, baked 132
Hare, smoked 102
Hazelnut-crumbed veal cutlets with eggplant relish 118
Hollandaise, thyme 83
Honey ice-cream 137
Horseradish, cream 34
    mashed potatoes 120

Hot, blood plum soufflé with
blood plum ice-cream 144,
143–4
butter waffles with grilled
peaches, vanilla bean ice-
cream & raspberry sauce
153
Hummus 164

Ice-cream, blood plum 144
honey 137
pistachio 147
toasted almond 138
vanilla bean 153
white chocolate & dried
blueberry 152

Jam, red onion 122
Jerusalem artichoke soup with
yabbies & sautéd apples 59

Kangaroo curry, red Thai 125
paillard of 123
prosciutto 76
King crab & BBQ pork
ricepaper rolls with
tamarind sauce 19

Lamb loin, roast 119
Leeks, marinated young 41
Lemon, cream 139
preserved 162
couscous 112
Lettuce, chilli pickled 7
Little pavs with clotted cream,
wild strawberries & rose
syrup 133
Liver, grilled calf's 95
parmesan crumbed calf's
103
Lobster salad with broad
beans, smoked tomatoes &
beet dressing 26

Mandarin & cardomom brûlée
145
Mango, chilli–, salsa 74
Marinated young leeks with
crab remoulade 41
Masala sauce 166
Mascarpone 146
potato, artichoke &, pie 68
Mayonnaise 159
chilli 124
tuna 29
Meringues, little pavlovas 133
Minestrone, squab 60
Mint pesto 119
Mocha sauce 167
Morels 84
Moreton Bay bug pizza with
coriander pesto 94, **92–3**
Mushroom, morels 84
wild, duck &, pastie 86
fricassée 102
Mussel & watercress salad 28
Mustard fruits 47

Ocean trout gravlax with
grilled corncakes &
snowpea foliage 35
Octopus, char-grilled baby 66
Oil, coriander 20
parmesan 21
truffle 49, 88
turmeric 36
white truffle 6
Okra, pickled 164
Olives 75
goat's cheese, fennel &,
tart 27
green, tapenade 47
Onion, red, jam 122
Orange, bittersweet, sauce 131
Ox fillet, peppered 120
Oysters 18
shooter 9

Pacific 8
Sydney rock, 7

Paillard, chicken breast with
preserved lemon couscous
& pistachio butter
112, **114–5**
kangaroo with sweet
potato mash & red pepper
chutney 123
Pancakes, potato 84
Pancetta 95
Pappardelle, sage 75
Parmesan crumbed calf's liver
with gorgonzola &
silverbeet 103
oil 21
Parsley sauce 39
Pasta, asparagus & fontina
tortelli 49
dough 161
prawn & basil ravioli 54
pumpkin tortellini 47
sage, pappardelle 75
Pastie, duck & wild mushroom
86
Pastry 138
cream 162
shortcrust 161
sweet 162
Pavlovas, little 133
Pawpaw, green, salad 82
Peaches, grilled 153
Pear, caramelised, pizza 146
spiced 87
Pepper, red, chutney 123
essence 110
sauce 27
terrine 28
roasted 164
stewed 29
Peppered ox fillet with
horseradish mashed

171

potatoes 120
Pesto, coriander 94
    mint 119
Pickled cucumber 34
    Okra 164
Pie, potato, artichoke &
    mascarpone 68
Pineapple, grilled 124
Pistachio butter 112
    crusted blue-eye cod with
    saffron mashed potatoes
    and masala sauce 111
Pistachio ice-cream 147
Pizza, banana & frangipane
    cream 137
    caramelised pear 146
    dough 161
    Moreton Bay bug 94
    sardine 89
Plum, ice-cream 144
    soufflé 144
Polenta 102
    gorgonzola 122
Poonie's icky sticky date &
    chocolate pudding with
    butterscotch sauce 155
Potato, artichoke &
    mascarpone pie 68
    galette 38
    horseradish mashed 120
    lattice chips 34
    mashed with truffle oil 88
    pancakes with
    sweetbreads & morels 84
    pink-eye chat 9
    pommes sarladaise 95
    saffron, gnocchi 69
    mashed 111
    salad, warm 104
    sweet, mash 123, 131
Prawn & basil ravioli with a
    smoked tomato sauce 54
    BBQ king 36

Preserved lemons 162
    couscous 112
Profiteroles with pistachio ice-
    cream & hot mocha
    sauce 147
Prosciutto 113
    kangaroo 76
Pudding, bread & butter 154
    Poonie's icky sticky date &
    chocolate 155
Pumpkin tortellini with mustard
    fruits & citrus
    butter 48, **52–3**
Purée, turnip 87

Quail sausage roll with verjus
    sauce 96, 98–9
    BBQ 83
    blackened 82
    roast 77

Raspberry, fig &, tart 138
    sauce 166
Ratatouille 56
Ravioli, prawn & basil 54
Red pepper terrine with mussel
    & watercress salad 28
    Thai peanut kangaroo
    curry with coconut rice 125
Relish, eggplant 118
Remoulade, crab 41
Rice, basil risotto 110
    beetroot risotto 76
    coconut 125
    spring pea 77
Ricepaper rolls, king crab &
    BBQ pork 19
Risotto, basil 110
    beetroot 76
    spring pea 77
Roast, duck breast on turnip
    purée with spiced pear 87
    with sweet potato mash,

bok choy and bittersweet
    orange sauce 131
    lamb loin with white beans
    & mint pesto 119
    quail & spring pea
    risotto 77
    Spring Bay scallops with
    tomato & cucumber
    salsa 14
    veal with tuna mayo &
    stewed peppers 29, 24–5
Roe, salmon 67
Roll, quail sausage 96
    ricepaper, king crab & BBQ
    pork 19
Root crisps 105
Rose syrup 133

Sabayon 136
Saffron mashed potatoes 111
    potato gnocchi with clams
    & asparagus 69, **72–3**
Sage pappardelle with duck
    ragout & olives 75, **78–9**
    roasted chicken breast with
    goat's cheese gnocchi 130,
    126–7
Salad, BBQ salmon Nicoise 40
    Caesar 15
    green pawpaw 82
    lobster 20
    mussel & watercress 28
    warm potato 104
    yabbie 38
Salmon, coulibiac of 67
    Nicoise salad 40
    roe 67
    seared salt-cured 88
    smoked, stack 34
Salsa, chilli–mango 74
    tomato 46
    tomato & cucumber 14
    verde 104

Sardine fillets, seared 47
    pizza with grilled eggplant tapenade 89
Sauce, bittersweet orange 131
    butterscotch 155
    gazpacho 38
    ginger 7
    masala 166
    mocha 167
    parsley 39
    raspberry 167
    red pepper 27
    salsa verde 104
    smoked tomato 54
    tamarind 19
    three-flavoured 105
    tomato 163
    verjus 96
Sausage roll, quail 96
Scallops, seared 61
    Spring Bay 14
Seafood, BBQ king prawns 36
    char-grilled octopus 66
    crab remoulade 41
    gnocchi with clams 69
    king crab & BBQ pork ricepaper rolls 19
    lobster salad 20
    Moreton Bay bug pizza 94
    mud crab 46
    mussel & watercress salad 28
    oysters 18
    shooter 9
    pacific oysters 8
    prawn & basil ravioli 54
    Spring Bay scallops 14
    steamed clams 58
    Sydney rock oysters 7
    yabbie salad 38
Seared salt-cured salmon on potatoes mashed with truffle oil 88, **90–1**

sardine fillets with a tomato–fennel stew & green olive tapenade 47, **50–1**
Sevruga caviar 6
Shortcake, blackberry 139
Shortcrust pastry 161
Silverbeet 103
Smoked salmon stack with pickled cucumber, horseradish & lattice chips 34, **30–1**
    tomatoes 26
Snails, sautéd 39
Snapper. whole deep-fried baby 105
Snowpea foliage 35
Soufflé, hot blood plum 144
    twice-baked roast garlic 39
Soup, chilled cauliflower 18
    roasted tomato 16
    chilli corn 58
    curried dhal 61
    Jerusalem artichoke 59
    squab minestrone 60
Spring pea risotto 77
Squab minestrone with Gruyère toasts 60, **64–5**
Steamed pink-eye chat potatoes with caviar & an oyster shooter 9
    wild barramundi on a basil risotto with red pepper essence 110, **108–9**
Stew, duck ragout 75
    tomato–fennel 47
Stock, chicken 158
    veal 158
Strawberries, wild 133
Sweet pastry 162
    potato mash 123, 131
Sweetbreads 84
Syrup, rose 133

Tabouleh 36
Tamarind sauce 19
Tapenade 165
    green olive 47
Tart, fig & raspberry 138
    goat's cheese, fennel & olive 27
Tartare, tuna 20
Terrine, red pepper 28
Thyme hollandaise 83
Toasts, gruyère 60
Tomato, & cucumber salsa 14
    concasse 163
    fennel stew 47
    salsa 46
    sauce 163
    soup, chilled 16
    smoked 26
    sauce 54
Tortellini, pumpkin 47
Trout, ocean, gravlax 35
Truffle oil 49, 88
Tuna carpaccio on shaved fennel with preserved lemon, sevruga caviar 6, **10–11**
    mayonnaise 29
    steak, BBQ 104
    tartare with eggplant crisps & coriander oil 20
Turmeric oil 36
Turnip purée 87
Twice-baked roast garlic soufflé with parsley sauce & sautéd snails 39

Vanilla bean ice-cream 153
Veal, cutlets, hazelnut-crumbed 118
    roast 29
    stock 158
Vegetables, char-grilled 66
    essence 49

fritto misto with tapenade, aioli and hummus 55
Venison burger with grilled pineapple & chilli mayo 124, **128–9**
Verjus sauce 96

Waffles, hot butter 153
Wasabi butter 8
Watercress, mussel & salad 28
White chocolate & dried blueberry ice-cream 'kreem between' 152, **148–9**
Whole deep-fried baby snapper with three-flavoured sauce & root crisps 105, **106–7**
Wild mushroom fricassée with smoked hare & polenta 102
Witlof, braised 113
Wood-fire roasted Pacific oysters with wasabi butter & brioche crumbs 8

Yabbie 16, 59
    salad with gazpacho sauce & galette potato 38, 42–3
Yoghurt, coriander 61

Zucchini flowers, stuffed, crisped 55
    fritters 83